Project Management Institute

IMPLEMENTING ORGANIZATIONAL PROJECT MANAGEMENT: A PRACTICE GUIDE

Library of Congress Cataloging-in-Publication Data

Implementing organizational project management: a practice guide / Project Management Institute.
    pages cm
 Includes bibliographical references.
 ISBN-13: 978-1-62825-035-0 (alk. paper)
 ISBN-10: 1-62825-035-6 (alk. paper)
1. Project management. I. Project Management Institute.
 HD69.P75I456 2014
 658.4'04--dc23

                              2013049609

ISBN: 978-1-62825-035-0

Published by:
    Project Management Institute, Inc.
    14 Campus Boulevard
    Newtown Square, Pennsylvania 19073-3299 USA
    Phone: +610-356-4600
    Fax: +610-356-4647
    Email: customercare@pmi.org
    Internet: www.PMI.org

PMI Publications welcomes corrections and comments on its books. Please feel free to send comments on typographical, formatting, or other errors. Simply make a copy of the relevant page of the book, mark the error, and send it to: Book Editor, PMI Publications, 14 Campus Boulevard, Newtown Square, PA 19073-3299 USA.

To inquire about discounts for resale or educational purposes, please contact the PMI Book Service Center.
    PMI Book Service Center
    P.O. Box 932683, Atlanta, GA 31193-2683 USA
    Phone: 1-866-276-4764 (within the U.S. or Canada) or +1-770-280-4129 (globally)
    Fax: +1-770-280-4113
    Email: info@bookorders.pmi.org

10 9 8 7 6 5 4 3 2 1

NOTICE

TABLE OF CONTENTS

LIST OF TABLE AND FIGURES

PREFACE

A Guide to the Project Management Body of Knowledge (PMBOK® Guide) – Fifth Edition and other PMI standards provide guidance on the management of projects, programs, and portfolios in order to achieve successful outcomes for those activities. In an organizational environment, projects, programs, or portfolios should be managed in alignment with organizational business strategy and objectives in a manner that will provide the most benefit to the organization.

Organizational project management (OPM) is the framework used to align project, program, and portfolio management practices with organizational strategy and objectives, and customizing or fitting these practices within the organization's context, situation, or structure. *Implementing Organizational Project Management: A Practice Guide* provides guidance to organizational management, PMO staff, and practitioners on these topics.

> *"Organizations with developed project management practices, benefits realization processes, portfolio management practices and program management practices and those with high organizational agility all have significantly better project outcomes than their counterparts who are less advanced in their project management practices."*

— (PMI's 2013 *Pulse of the Profession*™ p.11)

A practice guide is a new category in the PMI library of standards, which is intended to encourage discussion related to areas of practice where there may not yet be consensus. Practice guides are developed by leading experts in the field using a new process that provides reliable information and reduces the time required for development and distribution.

PMI defines a practice guide as a standards product that provides supporting supplemental information and instructions for the application of PMI standards. Practice guides are not full consensus-based standards and do not go through the exposure draft process. However, the resulting work may be introduced later as a potential standard and, if so, will then be subjected to PMI's documented process for the development of full consensus standards.

1

INTRODUCTION TO THE PRACTICE GUIDE

This practice guide is a resource for those who want to devise an integrated approach to managing an organization's portfolios, programs, and projects. This approach is based upon the management concept of organizational project management (OPM), which is described later in this section.

OPM advances organizational capability by developing and linking portfolio, program, and project management principles and practices with organizational enablers (e.g., structural, cultural, technological, and human resource practices) to support strategic goals. An organization measures its capabilities, then plans and implements improvements toward the systematic achievement of best practices.

This practice guide provides information and suggestions for creating useful OPM practices and methods, focusing on implementing and tailoring essential processes for organizational use, particularly in organizations that do not have a unified approach to managing the projects.

1.1 Overview of OPM Basics

"OPM is a strategy execution framework utilizing portfolio, program, and project management as well as organizational-enabling practices to consistently and predictably deliver organizational strategy leading to better performance, better results, and a sustainable competitive advantage" [1].[1] In short, OPM is the holistic management of portfolios, programs, and projects integrated with the organization's business management framework to deliver needed results. This strategy framework brings about balance and coordination, as Figure 1-1 reflects.

It is important to understand the relationship among portfolios, programs, and projects in order to understand OPM. A portfolio refers to a collection of projects, programs, subportfolios, and operations managed as a group to achieve strategic objectives. Programs are grouped within a portfolio and are comprised of subprograms, projects, or other work that are managed in a coordinated fashion in support of the portfolio. Individual projects that are either within or outside of a program are still considered part of a portfolio. Although the projects or programs within a portfolio may not necessarily be interdependent or directly related, they are linked to the organization's strategic plan by means of the organization's portfolio.

As Figure 1-2 illustrates, organizational strategies and priorities are linked and have relationships between portfolios and programs, and between programs and individual projects. Organizational planning impacts projects by means of project prioritization based on risk, funding, and other considerations relevant to the organization's strategic plan. Organizational planning can direct the management of resources, and provide support for the

---

[1] The numbers in brackets refer to the list of references at the end of this practice guide.

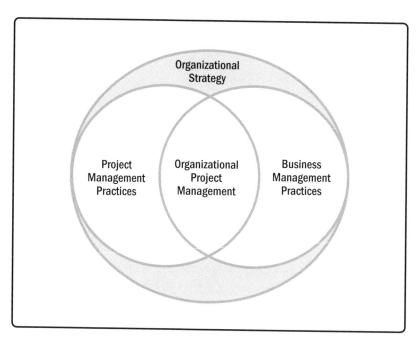

Figure 1-1. OPM Facilitates Efficiency between Project Management and Business Management Practices

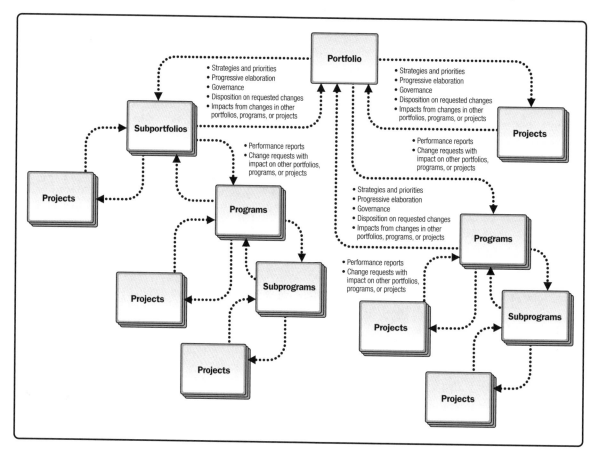

Figure 1-2. Portfolio, Program, and Project Management Interactions

component projects based on risk categories, specific lines of business, or general types of projects, such as infrastructure and process improvement. It is in this context that OPM exists.

Utilization of OPM has grown in the past 20 years, emerging from establishing good practices for a project, to establishing good practices for a program, and then to establishing portfolio, program, or project management offices (PMOs) for handling various aspects of support, coordination, and improvement. Some organizations adopt centers of excellence in order to coordinate OPM policy and competency development across multiple business units with PMOs. Many organizations have formalized the management of programs and projects, and in a growing number of cases, portfolio management. While some organizations have formalized practices, other organizations tend to manage projects in an ad hoc manner. In any case, projects are the common starting point when thinking about how to apply OPM, but the concept expands across the organization with the principle of engaging all necessary parts in the fulfillment of strategic goals dependent upon the program and project.

More organizations are beginning to realize that project management means more than having good project managers. An integrated leadership, management, and support environment is just as critical for the management of portfolios, programs, and projects as are other more traditional operational and support functions. Effective project management reduces unnecessary costs of doing business and leads to realized strategic objectives.

Project management, in terms of simply focusing on scope, time, and budget, is not sufficient for managing the scale and rate of change that is the norm in most organizations. Organizations that drive portfolio, program, and project management strategically with top management visibility use active executive sponsors on projects; consistent and standardized project management practices; methods to detect and cope with change effectively; and competent qualified project managers. Those organizations tend to be successful in delivering projects on time and on budget [2]. An OPM approach ensures that the portfolio aligns with the set of programs and/or projects that yield the appropriate value decisions and benefits for the organization. Portfolio reviews occur regularly and are adjusted as market conditions or strategy change. An analysis of the business impacts on the portfolio guides the portfolio review. The portfolio is adjusted, as needed, to deliver results or when other work makes it necessary to revise. These results directly link to business value realization. Feedback from value performance analysis influences the strategy of the organization.

1.2 Intended Audience for this Practice Guide

This practice guide is useful for organizations that would like to benefit from realizing their strategy through successfully implemented programs and projects that achieve intended benefits. This practice guide is intended for anyone who is involved in the oversight, design, management, appraisal, or performance and improvement of process, portfolio, program, and project results. This may include:

- Executives with responsibility for business divisions or business units;
- Executives or managers involved in the leadership, management, or oversight of programs and/or projects;
- Executives or managers responsible for developing OPM-related policies;
- Executives or managers involved in the support of organizational project management, such as those responsible for PMOs or centers of excellence;

- Senior program and project managers in leadership and liaison positions for OPM-related organizational capabilities; or

- Process and organizational change professionals (including quality assurance and capability management maturity improvement) who are involved with the design and implementation of portfolio, program, and project performance improvement initiatives.

1.3 Benefits of OPM to the Organization

OPM promotes the alignment of the organization's strategic objectives with related projects and their management, which many organizations consider to be a big benefit. Other attractive benefits are possible, as reflected in Figure 1-3.

Benefits tend to build incrementally. Organizational leaders should consider and carefully plan the selection, sequence, and realization of those expected benefits by investing in OPM practices.

Whether in the foundational or improvement stage of an OPM implementation, a benefits realization plan describing the steps, timing, and measures is needed to achieve organizational benefits effectively.

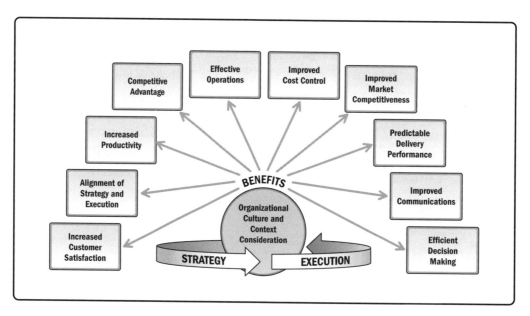

FIGURE 1-3. Potential OPM Benefits for Organizations

1.4 OPM Essentials for Implementation

Figure 1-4 represents the key elements that an organization needs to consider when implementing OPM. These implementation elements reflect current good practice in organizations that have undertaken the implementation of an OPM approach and realized success.

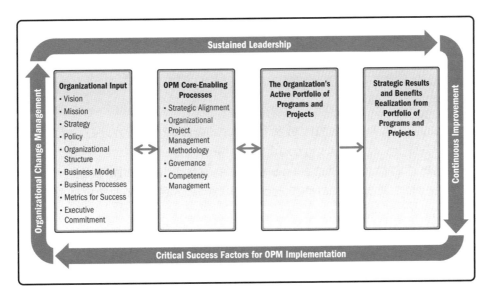

Figure 1-4. Essential Organizational Project Management Implementation Elements

The OPM core-enabling processes facilitate an organization's ability to realize its strategic objectives through portfolio, program, and project management. The strategic alignment process ensures programs and projects support strategic intent. Organizational project management methodology defines how people and the processes work to select and deliver portfolios, programs, and projects. Governance provides a framework in which organizations can make decisions that satisfy business needs and expectations. Competency management ensures that the right skills and knowledge are available to support OPM.

As elaborated in Section 2, critical success factors are sustained leadership, continuous improvement, and change management. Sustained leadership is required to establish and retain the efficacy of OPM in the organization. Continuous improvement draws upon audits, benchmarking, lessons learned, and other factors to identify what needs to be improved; for example, people and processes, oversight, goals and objectives, and organizational perspectives. Change management capabilities and the implementation of supporting change management strategies, plans, and activities are necessary to embed significant change in the organization.

Having a good OPM strategy execution framework assumes the involvement of all parts of an organization that directly or indirectly affect, or have a stake in, the selection, delivery, and outcomes of projects. OPM is a broader concept than portfolios, programs, or projects; however, these three domains are the focus of OPM to ensure that the organization optimizes its work to deliver strategy in order to realize the organization's vision or future state.

1.5 OPM Fit with the Organization's Business Model

OPM processes, methods, and practices, adapted to the organization, will fit with the business model, the structural organization, and various functions that constitute the organization. The term "fit" in the context of this practice guide refers to the organization's challenge to implement what is actually needed to create the value sought from its portfolios, programs, and projects.

Organizations may have some elements of OPM existing already, such as executive portfolio steering committees, sponsorship practices through the delegation of authority, project procurement support processes, project manager training courses, or documented project management practices and procedures. By formally instituting OPM, all of the necessary elements integrate appropriately for an effective system of project selection, execution, and delivery across the organization.

From a structural standpoint, the leadership of an OPM initiative or program should be in a central leadership unit close to or within the executive team, so it can coordinate OPM processes and methods with existing organizational processes. These leadership activities often are found in units such as enterprise project management offices (or centers of excellence), program management offices, and the varieties of project management offices found in today's project-oriented organizations.

1.6 Tailoring the Approach to Implementing OPM Core Processes in an Organization

Organizations need to address all of the key implementation elements by documenting how the organization will approach, plan for, and bring about desired related processes, practices, and tools to achieve fit. The organization will advance its OPM capabilities to the degree that makes sense for its business purpose and in the appropriate sequence. OPM advocates continuous improvement, therefore, the organization should have the ability to accommodate strategic shifts, new business models, changing markets, or new technologies.

The OPM policy and methodology that an organization uses are critical to establishing a system of practices, techniques, procedures, and rules used in portfolio, program, and project work to meet requirements and deliver benefits. OPM methodology speaks to all levels and facets of performing portfolios, programs, and projects. The other core-enabling processes facilitate the implementation of an OPM methodology. A well-planned OPM methodology makes appropriate and useful connections and modifications within the business model of the organization. The result is a tailored OPM methodology that evolves to support the organization over time.

Tailoring is the appropriate selection and alignment of organizational practices and methods for the value and types of projects the organization performs, which results in "fit." There are many dimensions of fit that each organization should consider carefully. Examples of important dimensions may include the following:

- A comprehensive, executive-led approach may be appropriate where there is a high degree of dependence on programs and projects for value delivery, rather than loosely managed functions or departments.

- A formal, defined and agreed-upon decision process may work better than an informal, nontransparent one when there is cross-functional involvement in major portfolio decisions.

- For organizations with multiple types of projects, it may be more efficient to align them to the appropriate levels of management rigor and governance by type, or group them in a program format, rather than using traditional grants of authority for functional or department managers.

Section 5 (Developing a Tailored Organizational Project Management Methodology) provides guidance that organizations can use to develop their own methodologies.

1.7 How to Use This Practice Guide

Figure 1-5 reflects the high-level input and outcomes of using this practice guide. In general, this practice guide is intended to assist organizational leaders with developing or improving an OPM framework that integrates the business model, the organizational culture, and this practice guide's elements and standards.

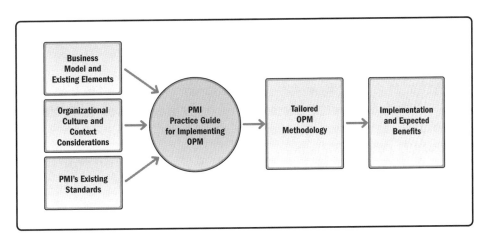

Figure 1-5. General Flow and Intended Outcomes of Using this Practice Guide

1.7.1 This Practice Guide and Related PMI Publications

It is important to note that PMI practice guides are intended to provide supporting, supplemental information and instruction for the application of PMI standards. Two key purposes of this practice guide are worth highlighting:

- This practice guide provides information that is unique but consistent with *Organizational Project Management Maturity Model (OPM3®)* – Third Edition. The following comparison between this practice guide and *OPM3* is provided to clarify their commonality and uniqueness:

  o This practice guide provides the processes that an organization can use to develop, implement, and improve OPM; *OPM3* provides a robust maturity model for use in assessing and enhancing an organization's OPM maturity.

  o Organizational enablers (OEs) are structural, cultural, technological, and human resource practices that can be leveraged to support and sustain the implementation of organizational project management. *OPM3* experts will notice that this practice guide focuses on four of the 18 organizational enablers identified in *OPM3* (see Appendix X2). Although all 18 are important, four are considered essential to implement and sustain OPM without necessitating a formal maturity assessment. By focusing on these four organizational enablers, this practice guide provides a foundation for organizations that are beginning to implement OPM. In addition, because this practice guide further elaborates on these four organizational enablers with process guidance, these four organizational enablers are referred to as "core-enabling processes" to reflect the added level of details.

○ In *OPM3*, Capabilities are formally defined as incremental steps leading to the attainment of one or more Best Practices. In this practice guide, capabilities are used more loosely to refer to the collection of people, processes, and technologies that enable an organization to deliver organizational project management.

- This practice guide is consistent with the current PMI standards for portfolio, program, and project management and *Managing Change in Organizations: A Practice Guide*.

1.7.2 How This Guide Is Organized

Section 1 (Introduction to the Practice Guide) provides the practitioner with basic concepts, principles, and definitions of OPM. OPM leaders can determine how these concepts, principles, and definitions relate to their organization's lexicon of related terms and activities. The organization maps the OPM components to the business model, noting the existing or missing OPM activity.

Section 2 (How to Prepare for an OPM Implementation) builds the case for OPM initiatives. This section is a resource for OPM leaders and senior management.

Section 3 (How to Implement and Improve OPM) describes the OPM implementation framework where the gap between the current state and desired future state is identified and the organization selects and implements initiatives to address this divergence and to move to the desired state. This section is a resource for OPM leaders and the implementation team to implement OPM for their organization. This section uses a change management approach within the OPM program structure.

Section 4 (How to Implement the Core-Enabling Processes) provides OPM leaders and senior management with the OPM implementation core-enabling processes necessary to facilitate an organization's ability to realize its strategic objectives through portfolio, program, and project management.

Section 5 (How to Develop a Tailored Organizational Project Management Methodology) provides OPM leaders with a process to create the organization's methodology for its portfolios, programs, and projects. This section offers guidance for tailoring processes and practices using management of a project as an example. The tailoring process, however, can be interpolated for portfolio and program management.

This practice guide helps organizations to identify and apply proven concepts, methods, and practices in order to realize and sustain OPM in the organization. It is intended to enable organizations to better structure the management of its portfolios, programs, and projects. This practice guide also refers to existing standards that organizations may want to include within their OPM context.

1.8 Summary

Section 1 covered the following points:

- OPM (portfolios, programs, and projects, collectively) plays a critical role in delivering the organization's strategy and intended benefits.

- When selecting, planning, implementing, governing, and delivering programs and projects, organizations that integrate OPM are more effective in achieving desired results than organizations that do not use this approach.

- Distinct processes and methods support the effectiveness of the application of OPM, which includes tailoring them to fit the organizational context.

- OPM is anchored in continuous improvement to help detect and react to change that inevitably affects the way in which an organization handles portfolios, programs, and projects.

2

HOW TO PREPARE FOR AN OPM IMPLEMENTATION

This section provides a high-level screening method for an organization to determine its readiness to implement OPM for the first time or improve an existing OPM implementation. By considering the items identified in this section, the organizational leadership can determine whether the conditions are appropriate to proceed with the establishment or revitalization of an OPM program. When some elements of OPM are present, these elements may be retained in the new OPM implementation as part of the overall improvement and will assist in building the business case, charter, and leadership team. Conversely, when negative conditions exist, such as insufficient senior management support to perform a robust OPM implementation, then smaller, incremental steps may be a more appropriate course of action.

Business and project functional areas need to focus on working together toward the same goals. This type of collaboration helps to minimize barriers created by a silo approach; for example, the lack of collaboration and standardization between business units. Prior to implementing an OPM program, the organization needs to determine its vision for a future state. Advance preparation helps to provide a better understanding of the business priorities, integrates business processes, and identifies areas of improvement, which will achieve greater alignment between projects and organizational strategy.

While a formal external assessment is not required, the use of a commercial project management maturity assessment may be useful. However, at some point, it may be helpful to leverage a maturity model to assist the organization map out a long-term, continuous improvement plan in a more established manner. A maturity model may be used to select specific areas of focus that will help the organization establish the starting OPM infrastructure and model. As the organization gains experience in OPM, an established and benchmarked maturity model can help to formalize an improvement path. *Organizational Project Management Maturity Model (OPM3®) – Third Edition* is a suggested resource [1].

2.1 Assess Readiness for OPM Implementation

Prior to launching an OPM program, the assessment of an organization's readiness for OPM measures the reality of the current organization in relation to its future state. The organizational systems, people, and culture should be assessed to determine whether they can support the change. While details on assessing change readiness can be found in *Managing Change in Organizations: A Practice Guide* [3], this section introduces a baseline of assessment elements. An appropriate executive leader of the organization's project management community, along with a small team of influential stakeholders, should take the following steps (see also Figure 2-1), which can be accomplished in parallel or in a linear progression.

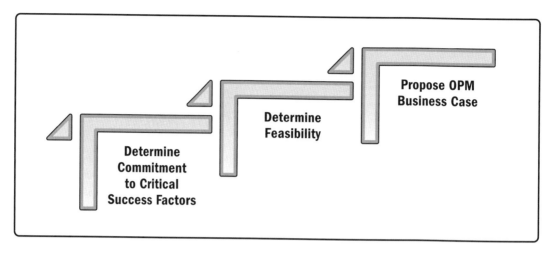

Figure 2-1. Basic Steps for Assessing Readiness

- **Step 1.** Determine the management commitment to the following critical success factors: sustained leadership, continuous improvement, and organizational change management (see Section 2.1.1).

- **Step 2.** Determine feasibility: share OPM information, assess current state and obtain consensus to the vision, and assess current organizational factors; then obtain consensus as to OPM feasibility (see Section 2.1.2).

- **Step 3.** Propose a business case for executive approval (see Section 2.1.3).

2.1.1 Step 1—Determine Commitment to Critical Success Factors

2.1.1.1 Sustained Leadership

In order to be successful, OPM requires a committed, sustained, executive-level leadership. Realistically, it is an ongoing program for as long as the organization performs portfolios, programs, and projects. There should also be an ongoing program (or organizational equivalent) dedicated to improving OPM. Consider how these activities could be created with regard to the organization's culture and structure.

Obtain full support and buy-in at the executive level to ensure OPM success. Executive sponsorship eases organizational change management challenges that arise when evolving and improving OPM. For companies starting from a low maturity of OPM, changing the organizational culture is one of the most important and difficult factors that will be encountered. The process to establish the alignment of business functions, including support functions, with an organizational approach to project management requires an advocate in the organization. It is preferable to select a member of the management team who has a strong knowledge of the organizational strategy and who will help to facilitate the activities for this purpose. Management buy-in as well as staff involvement is essential to support, administer, and monitor OPM efforts.

In addition to executive support, continued stewardship is also critical to the success of any long-term initiatives. Stewardship is performed by people who act as responsible owners by overseeing, protecting, and preserving OPM.

It is important to identify owners for OPM early in an organization's OPM program. Examples of owners include, but are not limited to, leaders of the OPM initiative, centers of excellence, portfolio or program management offices, and other senior OPM stakeholders.

If there is support and commitment to sustained leadership, then the initiative can move forward. If not, a means for cultivating the availability of sustained leadership should be explored.

2.1.1.2 Continuous Improvement

Long-term OPM success needs effective continuous improvement. Research indicates that many organizations have difficulty sustaining the value of any implementation [4]. This outcome occurs when incorrect expectations were established at the onset of the OPM program; for example, when a sponsor believes that the implementation is a one-time project rather than an ongoing program. After the early phase of implementing OPM, there is a point, as indicated in Figure 2-2, where the actions that an organization takes will either progress with continuous improvement on the upward curve or regress to a less-than-desirable level of competency, as indicated in the downward curve. The value OPM provides to the organization never remains flat or static as indicated by the lighter middle line in Figure 2-2, as there is always some change.

Sustaining the benefits of an OPM program requires funding, leadership, and continuous improvement focused on the OPM implementation effort and development outcomes. Continuous improvement starts with an initial assessment or benchmarking to determine the state of OPM and what improvements the organization needs to make to achieve this vision. The implementation plan includes periodic reassessments to measure progress and to detect any new organizational factors that may require adjustments to the OPM program. It is helpful to establish self-improvement efforts that include periodic reassessments to measure progress and to detect any new organizational factors that may require adjustments to the OPM program. Each of the successive iterations

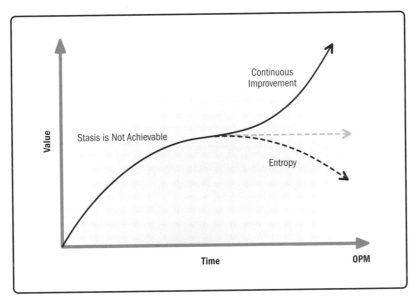

Figure 2-2. OPM Continuous Improvement (Adapted from *Researching the Value of Project Management*, p. 357 [4])

will have the benefit of the baseline metrics and established OPM processes to rely on, making it relatively easier to carry out improvements than it was in the initial implementation. A healthy practice is to refresh team members periodically without losing continuity. This helps to keep a current perspective of the needs of the organization, maintains the relevance of the improvements, and retains lessons learned.

An organization should proceed when there is a commitment to and capability for continuous improvement; otherwise, an organization should explore a means for cultivating that capability.

2.1.1.3 Organizational Change Management

To be successful with OPM, organizations need to be able to adapt and change, as necessary, to improve. OPM requires a commitment to and a capability for organizational change management. OPM implementation should be undertaken using the organization's change management approach. While improvement of project practitioner skills and methods helps an organization, many OPM benefits will require changes in the overall organization. This change entails an understanding across many stakeholders of the benefits that OPM will bring, and the ability to effect change, even for those who are negatively impacted.

An organization's ability to accept wide-reaching change should be evaluated as either a key factor in designing the approach or determining the scope and order of key changes. While details in change management practices are available in *Managing Change in Organizations: A Practice Guide* [3], some change management aspects to consider for OPM are as follows:

- Consider enthusiasm over time for the OPM-related changes. Organizations react differently to change, however the right approach can create the best environment for future change.

- Project practitioners may include influential people in the organization despite not being included in the decision-making process regarding OPM implementation.

- Leverage change management and communication skills from existing projects and programs within the organization to work with business stakeholders. This integrates existing project practitioners into the overall implementation.

- Develop a written change management plan, including a communications management plan, to establish an agreement with leadership to implement.

When there is a valid commitment and capability, proceed with organizational change management; otherwise, explore a means for cultivating that capability. Team involvement helps the organization develop a very clear depiction of the current state and potential implementations of an OPM strategy that maps directly to current business processes. It is important for the change management process to be accepted and driven by members of the organization.

2.1.2 Step 2—Determine Feasibility

Determine feasibility by identifying a strategic need to improve and evaluating the benefit of OPM improvement versus the cost. This high-level determination of whether or not it is feasible to promote OPM may include the following discussion items:

- Why is change needed?

- Why is OPM the solution?

- What will be considered a successful implementation?

- What needs to be accomplished when and by whom?

- Who needs to be involved in supporting the organization for a successful implementation and what will be their roles?

- What existing practices will be impacted? How will these practices be impacted?

- What are the expected benefits?

- How long is the OPM effort estimated to take?

- How much will it cost and what other non-financial resources will be required?

- What capabilities are required to initiate the change and do these capabilities exist in the organization?

- Are there other initiatives being executed that could impact an OPM initiative?

2.1.2.1 Share OPM Information

Communications regarding OPM and how it relates to the current organization is an ongoing OPM leadership responsibility, regardless of the organization's stage of OPM development. Provide training to stakeholders based on a competency/needs framework and implement checks to ensure the effectiveness of communication. Craft campaigns to inform OPM implementation team members and stakeholders by using briefings and targeted OPM training that may include topics such as:

- Explain OPM and what it will do for the organization.

- Identify gaps in the existing leadership culture.

- Mentor young leaders throughout the early stages of the process.

- Map OPM to the organization's current business processes, highlighting areas of improvement or areas to be looked at to achieve a future desired state.

- Describe the OPM framework and how it relates to the organization's business model.

- Describe the short-term and long-term benefits of OPM for the organization and employees.

- Depict the OPM roadmap for the next reasonable business planning cycle.

In the beginning, develop these communication elements with the knowledge that they will evolve over time as the program grows. Initially, these tools provide a platform to consult with all stakeholders as to their needs and requirements for establishing the OPM program or modifying their existing courses of action. Eventually, these communications will become part of the knowledge assets for the OPM program. Use the results of this communication exercise in order to gauge whether the OPM implementation should move forward, and if so, how to proceed.

2.1.2.2 Evaluate Current Organizational State

This activity informally captures current facts about the organization's OPM landscape, including cultural aspects, and helps to determine how best to formulate the business case for OPM.

Regarding OPM roles and responsibilities:

- Does the organization consider that managing projects requires professional skills?
- Does the organization have full-time project managers?
- Do projects have sponsors assigned to them and are those sponsors playing an active role in projects?

Accomplish these and other assessment topics by reviewing the organization's existing published information, credible sources, or knowledge assets. It is critical to understand the following organizational factors that can influence OPM success:

- **Strategic and portfolio adjustments.** What recent realignment has been made to the strategic plan that impacts portfolio priorities, assessments, and criteria?

- **Business results.** What is the current performance of contributing portfolios, programs, and projects? What is working and what needs to change? Are the business results in alignment with the organization's strategic objectives?

- **Environmental factors.** How do projects resonate with competitors, customers, or regulators?

- **Risk management.** What risk structures exist currently? Is the company more risk averse? What practices exist to balance programs between investment and risk? How quickly can the organization respond? Are benefits being tracked to verify return on investment? What is the organization's risk tolerance?

- **Skills and human resources.** Does the organization have the skills and resources to implement OPM? What career paths exist for portfolio, program, and project managers? What training and education exists?

- **Budget and resource.** Assess the budget and project landscape. What percentage of the budget is allocated for projects? What type of projects do they have, and how many projects are conducted per year? What is the project budget performance?

- **Organizational culture and style.** Are all involved parties consulted before a major decision that will affect them is made? Is communication informal or formal?

- **Change management.** How well does the organization handle change? Is the organization agile regarding change? What competing change initiatives could get in the way of an OPM initiative?

- **Organizational process assets.** What is the organization's governance process related to portfolios, programs, and projects? What exists for change, configuration, risk, and schedule management and their artifacts? How effective is the organization's project management information system? Are these organizational process assets integrated into programs and projects?

- **Organizational strategy, vision, and mission.** Are project managers and teams aware of the organization's strategy, vision, and mission? Are the projects strategically aligned?

- **Organizational structures, governance, rules, and policies.** What existing policies or organizational structures exist that may help or hinder OPM? Are there PMOs in place? Is there a formal or informal community of practice? Is the organization considered to be functional, matrix, or project-centric?

- **Program/project culture and style.** How many cross-functional projects exist? Is teamwork encouraged and how? Do team members (across all projects/functions) work together and brainstorm to refine their work processes? Does the organization invest time and resources on team-building exercises? Does the organization have any informal power circles and, if so, what is the balance of power between the organization's formal and informal circles?

- **Previous project management assessment results.** What credible knowledge does the organization have regarding capabilities and performance results relating to OPM?

- **Stakeholder engagement policy and procedure.** Who are the people/supporters/vendors/suppliers in the organization that need to be committed to OPM and what is the preferred method of communication?

Refer to Section 5 for additional questions to assist with tailoring OPM for a first-time implementation or improving an existing implementation.

When the leadership is satisfied that the necessary and sufficient information has been considered and shared, use the organization's customary procedures to determine the feasibility of moving forward with a business case. Include any information in this process, so that everyone understands what is at stake.

2.1.3 Step 3—Propose the OPM Business Case

Begin building the business case by organizing, presenting, and gaining executive authorization for OPM. Business case topics typically include:

- Executive summary,
- Problem statement or current situation,
- Alignment with business strategy,
- Key assumptions,
- Competitor OPM status or practices,
- Proposed approach and vision,
- Cost benefit analysis including resource considerations,
- Analysis of alternatives,
- Contingencies and dependencies,
- Benefit definition and measurement,

- Planned deliverables,

- Implementation roadmap or timeline,

- Opportunities and risks associated with not implementing OPM,

- Policy implications, and

- Recommendation(s).

The purpose of a business case is: (a) to capture the rationale for OPM using a cost-benefit and strategic planning model to reassure management that OPM is a worthwhile investment, (b) to set parameters and define success criteria, and (c) to provide a tool to guide the design, management, and evaluation of an OPM initiative. Initially, developing a good business case is instrumental in getting the OPM charter approved. Subsequently, a good business case provides critical data for the planning and implementation phases of OPM. Continuously reassess the assumptions that the business case is based upon to determine whether course corrections are needed to provide the intended benefit. When the assumptions no longer hold true (or will not hold true), revisit the business case using the new information and/or assumptions.

For long-term success of any initiative and to unify all parties involved, be sure to provide a compelling vision that drives all stakeholders to a shared desired outcome. Ensure that the vision paints a clear picture of a desired future state to be achieved by the initiative. In describing the vision for OPM, explain how OPM fits into the organization's long-term growth and strategy. Confirm alignment of the vision within the OPM business case, whenever practical.

Identify the benefits in OPM and how OPM will help the organization achieve its goals and objectives. Identify suitable metrics, key performance indicators, dashboards, and scorecards to demonstrate the impact of OPM. Include examples of tangible value statements that can be understood and realized. The potential benefits an organization may realize are identified in Section 1.3.

If a charter is required to proceed, base it on the guidance received from the business case. While the business case presents the options to senior leadership, the charter builds the detail from the approved business case course of actions with particular emphasis on time frames so that all stakeholders understand the ongoing nature of OPM. Typical elements of a charter include:

- Program vision, objective, and scope;

- Program structure, resourcing, and associated funding; and

- Risks and requirements.

Long-term success of OPM implementation requires approval and buy-in of the business case and charter from all stakeholders. Include all stakeholders at the earliest stages possible and keep them engaged throughout the planning and implementation path. To gain buy-in and consensus, make sure stakeholders are informed with all pertinent developments and issues so that they stay engaged.

2.2 Next Steps—Form the OPM Implementation Team

Use the approved business case and charter to establish the OPM program and the program management team. This will be an ongoing effort with continual improvement. As presented throughout this section, it is important to reiterate the key team elements: (1) executive sponsorship (which needs to be linked to the OPM implementation team) and (2) the need for the team to deliver change and provide continuous improvement. Staffing the team is dependent upon the circumstances of the organization. It should also be noted that one or more roles could be played by a single person. Consider staffing the following roles to support the OPM program: program manager, executive sponsor, process methodology expert, continuous improvement quality expert, (organizational) change management expert, quality assurance expert, communications specialist, and subject matter project managers and leaders. Establish an OPM program, consistent with *The Standard for Program Management* – Third Edition [5] or similar standard.

2.3 Summary

Organizations should apply the following principles presented in this section, ensuring that the concepts presented are clear:

- An OPM initiative should demonstrate and communicate clearly its linkage to the strategy, mission, vision, and goals of the organization.

- The business environment and culture should be considered carefully when implementing OPM.

- OPM leader(s) should be visible, fully committed, and openly supported by senior management.

- Important business strategies, values, and goals are distinctly associated with OPM.

- OPM leaders need to engage with all organizational stakeholders for their needs and requirements when mapping the breadth and pace of OPM implementation.

- There should be an approved OPM business case.

HOW TO IMPLEMENT AND IMPROVE OPM

In the previous section, senior management determined the organizational readiness for an OPM implementation, approved the business case, and formed an implementation team. This section describes the framework to implement an OPM foundation as well as OPM improvement.

The OPM implementation framework includes the activities and core-enabling processes that support the organizational leadership in aligning project management with other business management processes to achieve strategy. An OPM framework is implemented in three distinct phases and associated steps as outlined in Figure 3-1 and further described in this section. The implementation should be guided by executive sponsorship and carried out by an implementation team, as described in Section 2.2, comprised of a respected and skilled leader and team members from across the organization. It is important that the identified stakeholders act as official representatives for their groups and that they are empowered to act appropriately.

During this process, the gap between the current state and desired future state is identified. The organization defines and implements action plans to address divergence and move to the desired state. As the future state is reached or as the strategy changes, the OPM implementation phased process may need to be progressively elaborated to meet the new strategic plan requirements or to address divergence that may be overlooked during the process. A successful OPM implementation provides value to any organization when the implementation has the proper level of fit.

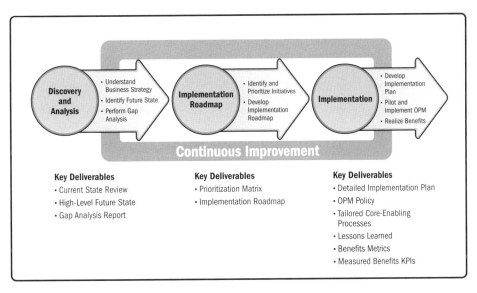

Figure 3-1. OPM Implementation Framework

3.1 Discovery and Analysis

Starting with the information from the readiness assessment (Section 2) as context, the OPM implementation team begins a discovery and analysis phase. This will help the team to gain an understanding of the organizational strategy and project management by identifying the current bond between projects and the organizational strategy and by outlining the resources and efforts required to work towards achievement of the organizational strategy. The key elements of this action are the documentation of the current state and the knowledge and ability to describe the future state and the requirements needed to fulfill it.

The discovery and analysis process is supported by the following steps:

- Understand the organization's strategy and project management practices (see Section 3.1.1),
- Identify the future state (see Section 3.1.2), and
- Perform gap analysis (see Section 3.1.3).

Each of the steps in this phase creates a deliverable that supports the efforts of the subsequent steps in the OPM implementation.

3.1.1 Understand the Organization's Strategy and Project Management Practices

Understanding the organization's strategy is one of the initial steps that serves as the main foundation during the OPM implementation. Gaining knowledge of the organization's strategy provides the basis for understanding the current state. Usually, a description of the organizational strategy is found in annual reports or in greater detail in internal and confidential documents.

Figure 3-2 depicts the relationship between organizational strategy and portfolios, programs, and projects.

The OPM implementation team should consider taking a holistic approach in order to gain a better understanding of the strategy and how the coordination of work between other functions in the organization will take place to achieve the strategy.

The main objective of OPM is to tie the project management processes to business processes and organizational strategy. It is important to understand how the elements of the business processes and organizational strategy relate to the elements of project management and how those elements can be mapped.

Figure 3-3 shows the dynamics of the relationship of the organizational strategy and project management. The portfolio includes those elements of the strategy that will be executed in the short- and long-term and those that are represented in programs and projects and other initiatives.

Programs and projects deliver results that progressively realize business value. During program and project execution, the impact to the business is monitored to ensure that the strategic objectives are fulfilled. Any variance is addressed during the portfolio review to make the necessary adjustments to the portfolio when strategy may be impacted by internal or external factors.

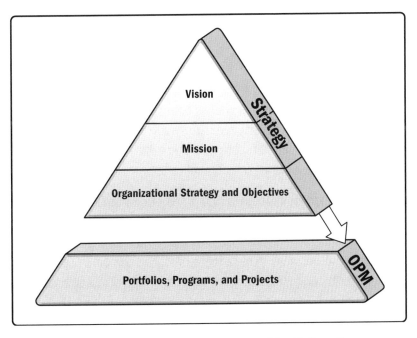

Figure 3-2. Relationship of Organizational Strategy and Portfolios, Programs, and Projects

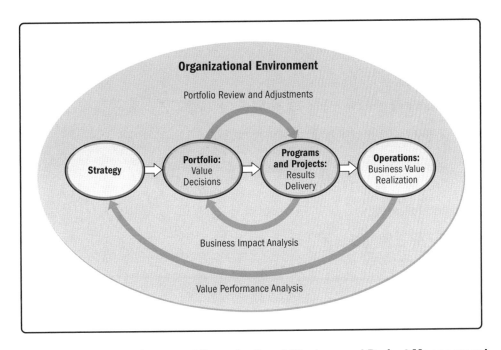

Figure 3-3. The OPM System of Organizational Strategy and Project Management

Portfolio, program, and project management are similar in that they align with or are driven by organizational strategies. Portfolio management aligns with organizational strategies by selecting the right programs, projects, and/or operational work; prioritizing the work; and providing the needed resources. Program management, however, harmonizes program and project components and controls interdependencies in order to realize identified benefits to support the strategy. Project management develops and implements plans to achieve a specific scope that is driven by the objectives of a portfolio or program, and ultimately, organizational strategies.

During this phase, the OPM implementation team identifies the current bond between project management practices and business management practices, as well as how they are aligned with the organizational strategy. This effort can be supported using the survey included in Appendix X3. The results of the survey provide valuable unbiased input to the OPM implementation team about the current state and reveal the divergence of the project management practices and the business management practices.

The strategic alignment core-enabling process supports the efforts of identifying the level of divergence and provides input to the gap analysis described in Section 3.1.3, which defines the tactical steps required to address the divergence. Figure 3-4 depicts four different scenarios that organizations may face. The ideal state is when both the project management and business management practices combine capabilities and best practices to implement improvements towards the systematic achievement of strategic goals, as depicted in quadrant 1 of Figure 3-4. Quadrants 2, 3, and 4 of Figure 3-4 show unsuitable scenarios that should be addressed in the gap analysis.

The OPM implementation team documents their findings and produces a current state review document describing how the organization works today, with descriptions of:

- Organizational structure and how it aligns with the organizational strategy,
- Organizational hierarchy,
- Core competencies,
- Project management processes and practices, including all variations of project management processes,
- List of all project management artifacts and templates,
- Business management practices,
- Key executive and management positions,
- Organizational functions,
- Organizational roles and responsibilities,
- Business processes,
- Cultural heuristics,
- Compete inventory of existing projects,
- Existing project performance data, and
- Relationships of current projects with organizational strategy.

It is important to mention that, initially, the information in the current state review serves as a baseline; however, it is a dynamic document and requires updates whenever internal or external changes affect the organizational strategy.

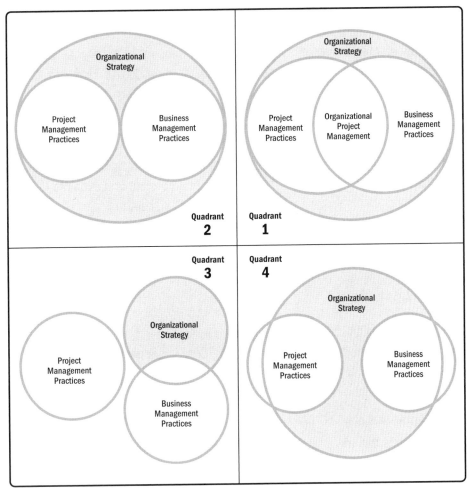

Figure 3-4. Levels of Divergence between Project Management and Business Management Practices

The deliverable from this step is the *current state review document.*

3.1.2 Identify Future State

Identify future state is the foundation of an OPM implementation. Upon completion of the current state review, coupled with an understanding of the long-term organizational goals, the OPM implementation team is ready to identify a high-level view of the future state of the organization and how competitive advantage can be created and sustained.

The current state review defines the starting point on the path to the future state. Using the information in the current state review, the OPM implementation team identifies the elements that will help the organization to perform better and strategically plans the execution of projects to achieve the future state. The desired future state is typically developed by the OPM implementation team and approved by senior management.

As described in Section 2.1.1, sustained leadership and continuous improvement are critical to the success of OPM. The amount of involvement from executive leadership directly correlates to the degree of success in implementing processes and executing strategic tasks. The support of core-enabling processes, such as competency management, strategic alignment, and governance processes, is indispensable in identifying and implementing the future state in the organization.

The high-level future state, developed by the OPM implementation team, provides valuable feedback to the organization on where changes need to happen and how soon they need to happen in order to achieve the organizational strategy. The high-level future state describes how the organization will work in the future and how changes will affect the organizational structure. The high-level future state is a dynamic document and requires updates whenever internal or external changes affect the organizational strategy.

The deliverable from this step is a *document describing the high-level future state of the organization.*

3.1.3 Perform Gap Analysis

Perform gap analysis bridges the current state, delivered in Section 3.1.1 (Understand Organizational Strategy and Project Management), with the future state. It helps the OPM implementation team to identify the variances between the current allocation and integration of resources with the required allocation and integration of resources in order to achieve the high-level future state.

There are many options available for performing a gap analysis. The implementation team can select from the available tools or artifacts that are a suitable fit for the organization. Survey results from Appendix X3 may be helpful in selecting the tools or artifacts to be used.

The gap analysis consolidates the outputs of the findings of the organizational strategy and project management of the future state to reveal areas that need to be improved to reduce the variance between the organization's business requirements and the organization's current capabilities. These elements serve as metrics when the suggested changes and improvements are implemented to compare the performance delivered by the future state versus the current state (which is the baseline for improvement).

Whenever possible, the gap analysis should use objective measurements based on the achievement of the future state and avoid inputting subjective assessments into the gap analysis model. In order to compare the performance of the current state to the future state, the OPM implementation team should meet with the required stakeholders and develop quantifiable metrics in tangible terms that will be comprehensible to the stakeholders involved in the analyzed perspective area.

The OPM implementation team conducts the gap analysis, which may cover the following areas:

- Organization's hierarchy (level of involvement of executive leadership),
- Organization's core competencies,
- Business direction,

3

- Business management practices,
- Review of existing metrics and alignment to future state,
- Project management practices and effectiveness,
- Project management competencies, and
- Project alignment with business management practices.

The support of organizational and OPM-enabling processes; for example, competency management, strategic alignment, and governance processes, is indispensable to development efforts of the gap analysis and the integration of its outcome with the rest of the organization, as deemed necessary.

Similar to the high-level future state, the gap analysis is a dynamic document and requires updates in the event that internal or external changes impact the organizational strategy.

The deliverable from this step is the *gap analysis report*.

3.2 Implementation Roadmap

Having completed the discovery and analysis phase and having a clear understanding of the gap to be addressed, the next phase is the identification and alignment of initiatives and development of an implementation roadmap for OPM.

3.2.1 Identify and Prioritize Initiatives

This step primarily uses the gap analysis data, and as needed, references the current-state review or high-level future state from the discovery and analysis phase to identify a list of initiatives that addresses the identified gap.

In the process of developing the list of OPM initiatives, focus on making a stronger tie to the organization's strategic objectives and metrics. These metrics provide the OPM implementation team with information to help in the selection and prioritization of initiatives to ensure alignment with the business case.

The initiatives resulting from the gap analysis are reviewed by a team of stakeholders and prioritized based on their strategic importance and difficulty in implementing, all of which are based on the current needs of the organization, fit, desired future state, resource-sharing issues with other projects and initiatives within the organization, business timelines, and strategy alignment. This process is essentially an application of program management, so be sure to follow the organization's program management practices. Refer to *The Standard for Program Management*.

To bring some objectivity and consistency to the prioritization process, first develop a set of weighted criteria that can be used to help prioritize the different initiatives. Then plot initiatives in the prioritization matrix based on the scoring.

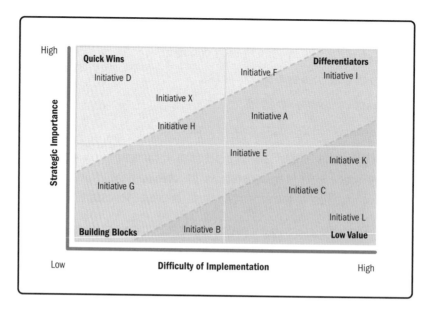

Figure 3-5. Example of OPM Implementation Prioritization Matrix

Plot the initiatives using a two-by-two quadrant based on the assigned priorities. An example of a prioritization matrix is shown in Figure 3-5.

Based on the prioritization ranking, the initiatives may fall in the following categories:

- **Quick wins.** These initiatives have high-strategic importance, are less difficult to implement, and can be completed within a short time span. These quick wins also help to achieve buy-in from the organization. Therefore, implement these initiatives immediately and include in the short-term planning.

- **Differentiators.** With high scores in the "difficulty of implementation" and "strategic importance" ranges, these initiatives will be the most complex to implement. Include these initiatives in long-term planning.

- **Building blocks.** These initiatives are easy to implement, but their contribution is minimal to the future state. Use a rigorous selection criterion to implement building blocks; otherwise, these initiatives could become distracters. Include selected building block initiatives in short-term planning.

- **Low value.** Do not implement these initiatives because they divert resources from higher-priority initiatives and may be too risky.

Develop the prioritization matrix as follows:

- **Review data.** Review the current state, high-level future state, and gap analysis data from the discovery **and analysis phase.**

- **Identify initiatives.** Identify a list of possible initiatives that can address the identified gap. Refer to Section 4 to identify the core-enabling processes to be selected as initiatives for inclusion in the current implementation roadmap. What fits one organization may not fit others; however, it is recommended that each organization implement all four core-enabling processes.

- **Define weighting criteria.** Define a set of weighting criteria for grading the initiatives to be included in the prioritization matrix to ensure consistency. Be sure to consider possible constraints, risks, opportunities, and the promised benefits from the business case in the weighting criteria.

- **Ensure alignment to strategy.** Assign a higher priority to the initiatives that can be directly linked to the organization's strategy. These initiatives support the achievement of the organization's strategy and do not contradict or conflict with the organization's strategy. Each initiative should move the organization closer to the future state by delivering benefits that close gaps identified in the gap analysis.

- **Identify collaboration and synergistic opportunities.** When possible, identify existing or impending projects within the organization that can benefit from shared scope, resources, etc. when linked or combined with a particular OPM initiative. In other words, apply a program management mindset when prioritizing these initiatives. It is also important to incorporate programs, projects, and other work that may be necessary to support a high-priority project.

- **Develop a prioritization matrix.** Using a prioritization matrix format similar to the example in Figure 3-5 or another preferred prioritization tool, plot the possible initiatives from the previous steps into a prioritized list.

- **Obtain agreement and approval.** Review the list with stakeholders and obtain agreement on the selected initiatives as well as their prioritization ranking. Obtain approval, as required.

The deliverable from this step is the *prioritization matrix*.

3.2.2 Develop Implementation Roadmap

Using the list of prioritized initiatives from the previous step, the team develops the implementation roadmap.

The implementation roadmap depicts the high-level, short-term and long-term milestones for implementing the required initiatives to achieve the future state. The implementation roadmap helps the implementation team to:

- View all initiatives, their estimated start and stop dates, and relationships to other initiatives, for example predecessor and successor relationships.

- Commit to implement the initiatives included in the roadmap.

- Forecast resources during the implementation of initiatives.

- Develop detailed implementation plans.

The implementation roadmap is a chronological representation in graphical form of the selected initiatives as well as a high-level view of key milestones and decision points. It depicts key dependencies between major milestones, communicates the linkage between the selected initiatives and business strategy, and provides a compelling vision and high-level snapshot of the supporting infrastructure and component plans.

Plot the initiatives in the prioritization matrix by grouping them, as required, and scheduling them based on priority, strategic importance, and timing of organizational resources and other collaborative opportunities. Figure 3-6 shows an example of a roadmap.

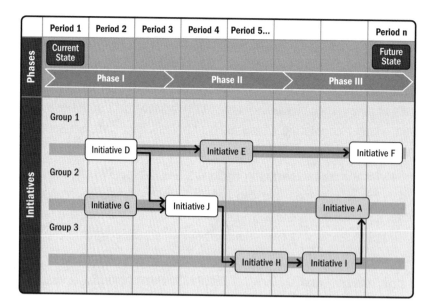

Figure 3-6. OPM Implementation Roadmap Example

OPM implementation is often a long-term endeavor with a starting point (the initial implementation), followed by an incremental improvement effort that can be handled as part of a routine annual planning process. A long-term implementation roadmap accommodates the strategy for sustaining OPM as a continuous, long-term improvement effort. In addition, the long-term view helps to gain leadership confidence and stakeholder buy-in because it: (a) is less threatening to the current commitments; and (b) demonstrates that OPM can be incorporated into the organization's long-term development strategy and implemented within a reasonable timeline.

While developing the implementation roadmap, consider taking a phased approach tailored to the needs of the organization. Examples of commonly exercised options include:

- **Implement by portfolio, program, and project domains.** This option can be used with the initial focus for all components of OPM associated with portfolio management, then program management, and finally project management. Depending on the needs of the organization, the sequence for implementation is flexible; however, it is likely that some level of formal or informal portfolio and/or program management is already in place to enable the selection and chartering of the organization's projects.

- **Implement by programs, projects, geographic locations, or organizational units.** This option considers the best logical grouping that coincides with the organizational structure.

- **Implement by readiness level and business impact.** This option is used when there may be substantial differences in readiness levels among business units, program groups, or projects. This option also works well when there is evidence that the business impact (positive or negative) can be managed by the timing of the OPM implementation. For example, if an organization decides to enter into a market where a formalized project management framework is required as a key entry criterion (e.g., a large defense contract) then the OPM implementation roadmap should reflect the appropriate timing.

- **Implement by maturity ratings.** This option is adopted by organizations that prefer a more comprehensive maturity-based focus in their OPM implementation approach. In this case, implementation is focused on business units, programs, or projects that have similar maturity model ratings or those that share the same target maturity ratings. Refer to the *Organizational Project Management Maturity Model (OPM3®) – Third Edition.*

Develop the implementation roadmap using the following activities:

- **Review the prioritization matrix.** Review the initiatives plotted on the prioritization matrix to gain an understanding of the identified initiatives and their relative ranking.

- **Select initiatives for implementation roadmap.** From the prioritization matrix, select initiatives for inclusion in the target planning cycle. For example, to develop a 5-year roadmap to match the organization's 5-year business planning cycle, select the number of prioritized initiatives that can be reasonably implemented during a 5-year cycle. Note that it is also possible to select all prioritized initiatives provided that the roadmap appropriately reflects the appropriate roadmap timeline.

- **Develop implementation roadmap.** Work with stakeholders to create a time-phased chart showing the following planning elements:

  o Planning period (year 1, year 2, etc.),

  o Long-term view for all selected initiatives as well as a short-term view for initiative(s) to be implemented in the most current planning period,

  o List of selected initiatives,

  o Alignment to associated strategic objectives, when applicable, and

  o Target start and completion dates for each initiative.

- **Obtain agreement and approval.** Work with stakeholders to obtain agreement and approval for the proposed implementation roadmap. Be sure to secure commitment for the required resources, budget, and proposed timing.

The deliverable from this step is the *implementation roadmap.*

3.3 Implementation

In the prior phase, the OPM implementation team prepared an implementation roadmap for OPM based on the output from the discovery and analysis phase. During the implementation phase, the OPM implementation team elaborates the roadmap into a detailed plan and carries out the plan to establish OPM in the organization (or implement OPM improvements). Depending on the scope and duration of the roadmap, it may require multiple cycles of implementation to complete.

3.3.1 Develop Implementation Plan

The first step in the implementation phase is to develop a detailed implementation plan for each initiative. While the roadmap lays out a long-term plan for the implementation of OPM, the implementation plan provides the details necessary to fulfill the roadmap.

Each organization that implements OPM starts from a different point and has a different desired target implementation. What fits one organization may not fit others; however, it is recommended that each organization implement all four core-enabling processes, as explained in Section 4 (OPM Implementation Core-Enabling Processes) while using the initiatives selected in Section 3.2 (Implementation Roadmap). A foundation of implementation guidance is provided in Section 4. There is also a vast knowledge base of good practices available to draw upon in PMI standards and other publications. The value to the organization in implementing OPM is maximized when the proper fit within the organization is achieved. This is why it is important to explore options before proceeding. Guidance in Section 4 should be used to elaborate the details of the implementation plan.

The OPM core-enabling processes are as follows:

- **Strategic alignment.** Strategic alignment aligns portfolios, programs, and projects with the organization's strategic goals and objectives.

- **Organizational project management methodology.** The system of practices, techniques, procedures, and rules used in portfolio, program, and project work to meet requirements and deliver benefits.

- **Governance.** The systems and methods by which OPM management and strategy are defined, authorized, monitored, and supported.

- **Competency management.** Competency management facilitates the timely and appropriate assessment of the skills and development of the experience necessary to implement portfolios, programs, and projects within the organization.

A significant step in an OPM implementation is the creation of an OPM policy (or amendments to an existing OPM policy) and determination as to which methodology, processes, and tools will be used to carry out the policy. The OPM policy formalizes OPM within the organization giving direction to members of the organization on what processes are required to be followed. Details for achieving this for each enabling process are outlined in Section 4. The OPM implementation team needs to decide whether they will be improving what is already in place in the organization or implementing something new. When implementing something new, determine whether to build it from scratch, buy it, or buy it and modify. In assessing which approach to take, consider the OPM budget and team size as the main determining factors. In each scenario, the underlying goal is to select the approach that will provide a high degree of fit with what will work best in the organization.

Consider using a pilot phase in the implementation plan prior to the implementation phase for each initiative planned, when the future state is substantially different from the current state. The pilot phase provides an opportunity to validate the fit of the implementation, reshape the organization-wide deployment, and gain buy-in from pilot participants throughout the organization. When the pilot is completed, initiate communications and training plans to support the implementation. This ensures that those affected have a clear understanding of what is new and how they should leverage it. Tailor the training so that it is specific to the organization. The detailed implementation plan provides an opportunity for adjustment in all plans after the review of pilot results.

The detailed implementation plan is comprised of a number of elements as described in *The Standard for Program Management* - Third Edition, which include a work breakdown structure and a program schedule. Create a work breakdown structure for implementing an OPM initiative using the following steps:

- **Determine requirements for initiative.** Beginning with the high-level input from the gap analysis performed in Section 3.1.3, document the detailed requirements for the initiative by elaborating the scope. Use the requirements to ensure that there is fit for the deployed initiative in the organization and include them as a subset of the success criteria for the initiative. When developing requirements, consider the following factors:

  o Characteristics of projects managed, for example, size, complexity, internal/external, duration, risk level, work content, and departmental/enterprise-wide applicability;

  o Characteristics of the organization, that is, formal/informal, matrix/functional, cultural mix, and/or global/colocated;

  o Budget;

  o Resource availability;

  o Current state of initiative components, such as project management methodologies, competency model, and artifacts;

  o Standards, such as *A Guide to the Project Management Body of Knowledge (PMBOK® Guide)* – Fifth Edition [6], other PMI standards, or industry-specific standards;

  o User-submitted requests for change;

  o OPM-related benchmark data; and

  o Lessons learned.

  For example, when implementing a training program for project managers in the organization, the requirements may include different levels of project management needed to support the organization's portfolio, the existing level of project management expertise in the organization, and the available learning tools available for training.

- **Develop tailored components of initiative.** These components may include a decision to buy or build for the initiative, based on the organization's current state, its ability to support different alternatives, and available resources. Once the decision is made, acquire, develop, and tailor the components for the initiative. When the organization is improving an existing deployed initiative, a pilot phase may not be needed.

  For example, an organization may choose to hire a learning provider to deliver an off-the-shelf training program or may choose to develop a company-specific training program. In either case, this activity should result in a set of learning tools that can be piloted.

  o *Pilot initiative.* Develop a pilot for the initiative before widespread implementation to minimize risk across the organization and to ensure a successful implementation. The pilot may be either a subset of the initiative across a large part of the organization or a full initiative across a small part of the organization. In either case, the goal is to ease the organization through the process of change without introducing unnecessary risk. For example, provide training to project managers in one department and assess the results before proceeding with a complete deployment.

  o *Adjust components of initiative and implementation plan.* Based on lessons learned during the pilot, review all plans for implementation and adjust accordingly. This may include adjustments to specific requirements for the initiatives or the deployment process. For example, the pilot may reveal that the practitioners being trained in project management also need additional training in team leadership. To fill this gap, the implementation team could supplement the planned training. In this case, the planned schedule needs to be adjusted to accommodate the additional time needed for training.

○ *Deploy initiative across organization.* Finally, based on the implementation plan, deploy the initiative fully across the organization. For example, conduct the training for all project managers in the organization.

○ *Conduct lessons learned review.* Throughout the implementation, the team should identify lessons learned (during meetings, as deliverables are completed, etc.). At the conclusion of each implementation phase, conduct a thorough review to compile a repository of the lessons learned. For example, assess the progress made in improving project management skills across the organization to determine any remaining gaps and to understand how to keep the level of knowledge current as the organization changes in the future due to turnover, business changes, etc.

Base the detailed implementation plan on good program management practices and include all of the subordinate plans that comprise a complete program management plan. The implementation plan should include a clear schedule that includes deliverables, due dates, and responsibilities, and should incorporate steering committee meetings. While not all-inclusive, consider the following for developing components of the program management plan, which are specific to implementing OPM:

- **Benefits realization plan.** The benefits realization plan identifies how and when the selected benefits of OPM will be delivered to the organization. The baseline document guides the delivery of benefits during performance of the detailed implementation plan. Executive support for OPM may fade when the implementation team is unable to demonstrate benefits from its implementation.

- **Resource management plan.** Develop a plan for identifying, securing, and managing OPM core resources. This includes a possible organizational reporting structure of the team and resource commitment. When an organization does not have a dedicated team of OPM practitioners or has limited funding to support such a team, one alternative approach is to enlist volunteers from the project management community in the organization for the effort. The OPM implementation team should work with management to create incentives for participation as a volunteer in the OPM implementation. The incentives are easily offset by the community buy-in that results when volunteers socialize their experience into the community. Another approach, especially when the organization is conducting an OPM implementation for the first time or is a low-maturity organization, is to engage OPM subject matter experts knowledgeable in OPM models, standards, and practical approaches that enhance and accelerate organizational benefits.

- **Organizational change management plan.** Organizations assess change readiness, initiate change, and manage change for initiatives that modify their environment, processes, and tools. Organizations achieve successful change initiatives with a clear understanding of the current state and desired state, coupled with effective management and leadership of the process and human factors. An OPM-detailed implementation plan should emphasize the people element of change, in addition to the technical aspects. An effective plan ensures people have a good understanding of how the changes will affect their job and specifies the skills and capabilities for applying the changes to produce the desired results.

Change management is more than just communication management. Effective organizational change management requires an understanding of stakeholder attitudes toward the change and ensures the proper training, support, and reinforcement for all involved.

- **Risk management plan.** Effective management of OPM implementation also requires effective management of possible risks to the OPM implementation program and secondary risks caused by OPM that may affect the organization. This process should also seek to find opportunities for improved implementation. Identify the risks and plan for mitigation using a standard risk management process.

- **Key performance indicators (KPIs).** Define KPIs for performance tracking. The starting point for these KPIs is the business case that was available from the early OPM effort, with details developed as part of the planning process and data collected and measured with refinements incorporated as part of the OPM implementation. These will become the metrics for measuring delivery of expected benefits; therefore, it is important to capture a baseline prior to the OPM implementation in order to determine to what extent OPM has improved the KPI.

The deliverable from this step is a *detailed implementation plan*.

3.3.2 Pilot and Implement OPM

The pilot and implement step of OPM consists of carrying out the detailed implementation plan developed in the previous step. If one or more pilots are planned, the OPM implementation team should adjust the detailed implementation plan after the pilot(s) are concluded, based on lessons learned. A pilot may not be necessary or appropriate in all OPM implementations.

Implementing OPM can be a lengthy endeavor and often stakeholders are impatient and are only interested in progress that can be seen "this month" or "this quarter." If stakeholders do not see progress, they may become disinterested in the program and could pull support, funding, etc. An OPM implementation program should strive to attain quick wins in small steps early in the cycle. Quick wins should be celebrated with the team, widely communicated, and used as part of the organizational change management plan to promote the value of OPM. This is especially true when an organization does not have any formalized project management processes in place. If a large ambitious OPM process improvement is desired, it may be best to implement it in smaller steps, both for the benefit of those implementing the improvements and for the ability to show short-term successes. This does not imply a reduction in the final desired outcome, but rather an incremental approach to achieving it. While this decision is a primary objective of the implementation roadmap, the OPM implementation team should evaluate pilot results to ascertain whether rework of the implementation roadmap is necessary.

In some organizations, it may be useful to classify project and programs, and offer different levels of OPM process rigor to support different levels of complexity, size, duration, etc. While fit at an organizational level is important, it is also important to achieve the correct level of fit at the program or project level. Too much rigor will be perceived as administrative overhead. Too little rigor will likely inhibit achieving the desired OPM goals. This is another area of the OPM implementation program that may be adjusted, based on the results of pilots in different parts of the organization.

Once the pilot is completed and any adjustments are made from lessons learned, the OPM sponsor should work with the organization's executive stakeholders to ensure that a new OPM policy is documented and communicated clearly, concisely, and emphatically to all affected stakeholders in the organization. In some organizations, this may be accomplished through communications from the head of the organization. In other more complex organizations, it may be necessary to use formalized documentation that is distributed at various levels in the organization from recognizable executives. The key is to ensure that everyone understands that a change has occurred, what it means to them, and what actions they need to take. It needs to become important enough so that stakeholders will prioritize it over other activities occurring in their daily job. The organizational change management plan frames the steps needed to accomplish this, including the plan for communications, as well as training. The OPM policy should be available in a prominent location, such as an intranet webpage along with other organizational policies.

The deliverables from this step are *OPM policy, tailored core-enabling processes, lessons learned, and benefits metrics.*

3.3.3 Realize Benefits

As the detailed implementation plan is carried out and OPM is incorporated into the organization, the organization will begin to realize the intended benefits, as defined in the benefits realization plan. In order to determine whether the intended OPM organizational benefits are being realized, the OPM implementation team needs to measure progress according to the defined quantitative KPIs.

Depending on the size and complexity of the organization, there are tactical and strategic approaches to measuring progress. From a tactical perspective, a scorecard can be used with OPM metrics to measure the progress of specific components of an enabling process. Examples of scorecard measurements are the percentage of project managers in each internal organization that have attained the desired level of education for their position, or a grading scale for what percentage constitutes red, amber, or green. This type of metric is valuable for the OPM implementation team and shows progress against their tactical program goals. This type of metric is most useful in the beginning stages of an OPM implementation, but may not be suitable for the business leaders to accept as evidence of benefits realization.

Measuring the business impact from an OPM implementation is the best way to show business leaders the value of the OPM implementation. This is also the most challenging metric to incorporate. Business leaders are interested in business results that affect the bottom line, such as time to market, budget attainment, and resource utilization, etc., including other metrics that directly measure the organization's attainment of its strategy. For example, it may be possible to take a project management specific indicator, such as the increase in projects completed on time, and associate it with a business value indicator, such as time to market, to determine a financial value to the business.

The challenge is that most measurements for business results are impacted by many internal and external factors beyond the implementation of OPM. For this reason, it is important to have a baseline measurement for any business value indicator that the business leaders understand and accept as a starting point. Many OPM implementations fail to show value to business leaders because measurements are not taken until the core-enabling processes are in place. Agreement on a baseline KPI measure is a critical success factor in demonstrating the value of OPM.

Experience has shown that a measurement program should start with basic measures and evolve into models that are more complex over time with application and feedback from stakeholders.

The deliverable from this step is the *measured benefits KPIs*.

3.4 Continuous Improvement

Continued realization of OPM benefits is dependent upon the stewardship of the OPM governance body in the organization. As explained in Section 2, studies have shown that the majority of organizations that do not pursue continued improvement will regress and lose the value previously attained. For that reason, it is important to ensure that the OPM policy outlines a continuous improvement process.

It is recommended that the OPM cycle be continued in the organization on an ongoing basis. Conduct the analysis and discovery step periodically (for example, every 12 to 18 months) to determine the state of OPM and to identify which improvements should be made, and then follow up with the remaining cycle phases described in Section 3. Each successive iteration that is conducted through the cycle has the benefit of the baseline metrics and OPM processes to rely on, making it easier to carry out than the initial implementation cycle. It is valuable to cycle different project management professionals into the assessment teams when the organization is large enough to support it. When this is done, insight is maintained in the process and is grounded in what is being practiced, rather than relying solely on dedicated OPM implementation team members who, over time, may become disconnected from the practice of project management in the business. This practice also serves to reinforce a deeper understanding of OPM and its importance, and builds more champions across the organization.

3.5 Summary

3.5.1 Discovery and Analysis

- The current state review documents form a basis for a common understanding of the strategy, business management processes, and project management processes.
- The high-level future state describes the desired end state, including the effective alignment of the business and project management processes to the strategy.
- Gap analysis describes the variance between the current state and the future state with suggested areas of work needed to achieve the future state.

3.5.2 Implementation Roadmap

- Using the information from the gap analysis, the implementation team develops a list of OPM-related initiatives, then identifies and prioritizes the initiatives to align with the organizational strategy.
- The implementation team develops an implementation roadmap that considers the current business constraints.

3.5.3 Implementation

- The implementation team develops detailed implementation plans for each initiative based on the roadmap and gap analysis, including appropriate subordinate plans and implementation schedules.
- The OPM benefits realization plan provides a consistent means of collecting and reporting the KPIs of OPM, which can be used to feed back into the continuous improvement of OPM.

3.5.4 Continuous Improvement

- Continued realization of OPM benefits is dependent on the continued pursuit of improvement.
- The OPM governance body is responsible for the stewardship of OPM and a continuous improvement process as part of the OPM policy.

HOW TO IMPLEMENT THE CORE-ENABLING PROCESSES

The OPM implementation core-enabling processes facilitate an organization's ability to realize its strategic objectives through portfolio, program, and project management. This practice guide focuses on four OPM implementation core-enabling processes: competency management, governance, OPM methodology, and strategic alignment. These key components of OPM are depicted in Figure 4-1. Competency management ensures that skills are developed and available when needed to implement a portfolio, program, or project. Governance describes the decision-making framework and oversees the work done for each process. Organizational project management methodology provides the structure (people and processes) necessary to implement portfolios, programs, and projects. Strategic alignment aligns portfolios, programs, and projects with business strategy. Each core-enabling process is essential for delivering an organization's strategic objectives utilizing OPM. However, all organizations are unique and should consider what level of implementation is appropriate given their current and desired state of maturity. Maturing organizations can also use *OPM3* as a comprehensive maturity model based upon an expanded list of 18 enablers, which includes the four OPM implementation core-enabling processes discussed herein.

Methodologies and processes for each core-enabling process should be tailored to fit each organization's needs using the OPM implementation framework discussed in Section 3. Specific guidance and an example of how to develop a tailored organizational project management methodology is further explained in Section 5.

This section describes the organization's requirements when it is operating at a foundational or improved level. Organizations at the foundational level are just beginning to implement OPM; therefore, do not have a defined

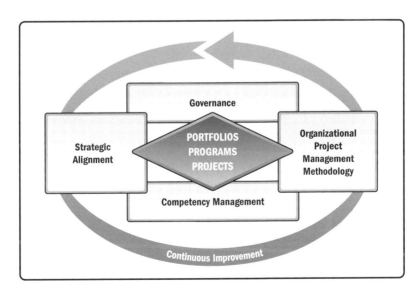

Figure 4-1. Core-Enabling Processes

approach for managing portfolios, programs, or projects. The foundational level outlines the basic steps for an OPM implementation. The improved level expands on the foundational level to provide a more robust or mature OPM implementation. Organizations should consider all four core-enabling processes when implementing OPM. The processes presented in this section are as follows:

Section 4.1 Strategic Alignment

Section 4.2 Organizational Project Management Methodology

Section 4.3 Governance

Section 4.4 Competency Management

4.1 Strategic Alignment

Aligning projects, programs, and portfolios with the organization's strategic objectives and goals is the purpose of strategic alignment. To simplify the explanation in the following discussion, reference to the term portfolio is inclusive of programs and projects in the context of this core-enabling process.

Strategic alignment, supported by governance, enables organizations to consistently manage and align portfolios with business strategy to maximize the value of portfolio outcomes. As an organization develops its strategy, there is typically an evaluation and selection process that helps the organization to determine which portfolios to approve, deny, or defer.

Whether formally or informally, an organization selects and authorizes the initiatives it wishes to implement. The more capable an organization is in terms of OPM, the more likely it is to have a formalized selection process and governance body to define the strategic objectives and benefits a particular portfolio is expected to deliver. In addition, an OPM-enabled organization is more likely to utilize an enterprise risk and opportunity management process to enhance strategic alignment.

Strategic alignment includes the processes used to couple the organizational strategy to the inventory of portfolios, along with the organizational structure, resources (e.g., human, financial, material, equipment), and organizational process assets in order to establish a balanced, workable plan. Key performance indicators are monitored against the organizational strategy, goals, and objectives. Performance feedback provides input to recommend improvements to strategy and goals or changes to portfolios.

4.1.1 How to Plan and Implement Strategic Alignment

The following topics provide a general discussion of how to plan for and implement strategic alignment:

The inputs for planning and implementing strategic alignment include

- Organizational strategy and objectives,
- Inventory of portfolios and/or associated roadmaps,

- Organizational structure,

- Organizational resources (e.g., human, financial, material, and equipment),

- Organizational process assets (e.g., policies, procedures, and lessons learned), and

- Benchmark data for market and regulatory expectations, industry, and competitors.

Outputs, some of which may already exist, from planning and implementing strategic alignment include:

- Strategic plan alignment, validation, and recommendations for improvement;

- Prioritized and optimized inventory of portfolios;

- Portfolio charters;

- Resource investment plans; and

- Key performance indicators and measures of portfolio success, traceable back to organizational strategy.

For a more in-depth discussion of managing portfolios, programs, and projects in a strategic alignment context, refer to *The Standard for Portfolio Management* – Third Edition [7], *The Standard for Program Management* – Third Edition, *A Guide to the Project Management Body of Knowledge (PMBOK® Guide)* – Fifth Edition, and the *Organizational Project Management Maturity Model (OPM3®)* – Third Edition.

4.1.2 Foundational Strategic Alignment

An organization that is at an early maturity level of implementing OPM should focus initially on identifying basic business objective(s), existing portfolios, and a list of responsible positions or functions within the organization. It is recommended that a team be assigned to implement strategic alignment. The organization may also want to consider using expert guidance during the first phases of this process. For an organization that is beginning to implement OPM, the following foundational activities are needed to initiate strategic alignment planning:

- Identify strategic objectives and goals.

- Take inventory of the active portfolios.

- Identify responsible organizational positions or functions for achieving business goals and objectives.

- Identify responsible organizational positions or functions and available resources (e.g., human, financial, material, and equipment) for the current inventory of portfolios.

Using these foundational strategic alignment planning elements, the organization should conduct the following foundational actions:

- Study the strategic plan and the high-level organizational investment decisions that could affect implementation of the objectives. Note the organizational positions or functions responsible for achieving business goals and objectives.

- Develop an inventory of portfolios aligned to the strategic plans, goals, and objectives. Base this inventory on the existing portfolios, programs, and projects that support attainment of the organizational strategy. Be aware that it may take more than one pass at developing the inventory to collect sufficient facts to determine whether the portfolio is fully, partially, or not aligned. Portfolios that do not align with organizational strategy may need to be modified to align with the organization's goals and objectives.

- Develop and formalize portfolio charters that align with the strategic plan and are authorized to continue. The charters should identify the organizational positions or functions responsible for the approved inventory of portfolios.

4.1.3 Improved Strategic Alignment

Improving strategic alignment ensures that an organization's planned portfolios align with its strategic objectives and requires organizational resources to be available prior to approval. The organization applies a process of continuous improvement using key performance indicators to reassess and recommend improvements to its strategic goals and objectives, the corresponding alignment of portfolios, and organizational resources to ensure maximization of value. Coupled with this, an OPM-capable organization may use enterprise risk management as a means for strategic alignment by assessing risks and opportunities and using mitigating actions to help address alignment gaps.

In addition to the foundational elements discussed in Section 4.1.2, the following additional elements are appropriate for an organization improving its strategic alignment:

- Take inventory of planned portfolios not yet approved.
- Identify organizational positions or functions responsible for planning portfolios and associated leadership responsible for approving the initiative.
- Identify organizational resources (e.g., human, financial, material, and equipment) that are available, required, and being used for portfolios that are planned and approved.
- Identify available organizational process assets that may be utilized for planning, chartering, and accomplishing portfolios.
- Identify the organization's policies and procedures for organizational enablers (e.g., purchasing, HR, capital, risk tolerance, and other applicable policies) that facilitate business process integration.
- Identify key performance indicators that are measured against recommended improvements to align to OPM and validate portfolio success, attainment of strategic goals and objectives, and optimal use and enhancement of resources.

Using these additional strategic alignment planning elements and the products identified in Section 4.1.2, the organization striving to improve OPM should implement the following additional actions:

- Update the inventory of aligned portfolios to include the inventory of planned portfolios that have been determined to be in alignment with organizational strategy.
- Utilize available organizational and portfolio process assets for planning and chartering proposed portfolios.

- Update or develop portfolio charters for the inventory of planned portfolios that align with the strategic plan and are authorized to continue. These charters should identify the organizational elements responsible for working these newly approved portfolios, and the organizational resources (e.g., human, financial, material, and equipment) available, required, and being used to plan and achieve the portfolio objectives. The responsible leadership approves these charters.

- Utilize available organizational process assets to take programs and projects to a successful conclusion.

- Develop KPIs to measure attainment of organizational goals and objectives, strategic alignment and performance of the portfolio, resource utilization, and effectiveness of organizational process assets.

- Analyze the KPIs in use and determine if they are adequate or if it is necessary to make any improvements.

- Perform a gap analysis to compare the portfolio inventory and organizational resources with the strategic direction and the organizational investment decisions. This is essential to properly manage strategic change.

- Develop and use a simple prioritization model with weighted criteria or ranking by quantifiable benefits to ensure alignment to organizational strategy and objectives, expected return on investment, risk, and dependencies.

- Using results from this gap analysis and prioritization model:

    o Identify recommendations for possible improvement in organizational strategy and objectives.

    o Prioritize, optimize, and update the inventory of portfolios aligned with changes in strategic plans, goals, and objectives.

    o Identify and implement corresponding enhancements to the organizational resources and organizational process assets.

- Integrate strategic alignment with the organization's risk management processes to identify, assess, and manage risks and opportunities, including mitigation measures, against strategic goals and objectives.

4.1.4 KPIs for Strategic Alignment

KPIs should be developed and used to assess an organization's strategic alignment, and to the extent practical, should look outward at risks and opportunities on the horizon which can impact an organization's performance. At the organizational level, a balance of financial and nonfinancial KPIs should be established which will be critical to assessing the health and performance of an organization.

KPIs are used to assess whether expectations are clearly defined and accountabilities are aligned with strategic priorities, and can be used to measure personnel commitment to or understanding of an organization's mission, vision, and objectives. Additional KPIs can be implemented to ensure that the organization's efforts and rewards are aligned and to assess management of the portfolios, programs, and projects. For example, establish a KPI to assess management by measuring the number of portfolios, programs, and projects reviewed using stage-gate analysis. Care should be taken to avoid too many KPIs, which may result in misalignment or incompatibility of KPIs within an organization.

4.2 Organizational Project Management Methodology

Organizational project management methodology describes a system of practices, techniques, procedures, and rules used in portfolio, program, and project work to meet requirements and deliver benefits to support the organization's strategy.

The methodology should be tailored and scaled to meet the needs of the organization. This varies organization-by-organization, or division-by-division, based on culture, size, and maturity. This methodology utilizes existing organizational process assets to provide an organization-specific structure and guidance that improves the success of portfolio, program, and project completion. An organization could have single or multiple methodologies in use.

Organizational project management methodology connects critical parts of the organization. A well-defined methodology makes appropriate and useful connections with the business model of the organization.

4.2.1 How to Plan and Implement an Organizational Project Management Methodology

Organizational project management methodology implementation consists of identifying existing organization-specific inputs and developing a set of plans and processes to achieve the desired project management methodology state.

The inputs of this activity include:

- Understanding the project types that the organization will manage, for example, global, technology, or construction projects. Understanding project types is important to designing a project management methodology that fits the organization's needs.

- Recognizing the relative size of projects that will be managed. Organizations that only manage small projects may need less sophisticated processes and methods.

- Understanding existing internal and external supporting organizational processes and procedures and other organizational attributes for use as references and call outs from the methodology.

- Compiling historical data on completed programs and projects within the organization that may be excellent sources for good practice templates and forms.

- Documenting project lessons learned to extract good practices to avoid pitfalls.

- Identifying an archive repository to save original versions of existing project management methodology collateral as appropriate.

The outputs of this activity include (and note that some elements of these may already exist):

- Project management methodology;

- Changes to current policies and procedures and proposed new policies and procedures;

- Project document templates;

- Project roles and responsibilities;

©2014 Project Management Institute. *Implementing Organizational Project Management: A Practice Guide*

- Portfolio view of portfolios, programs, and projects;

- KPI visibility to drive corrective and continuous improvement actions; and

- Updated organizational change management plan, communications management plan, and training plan (refer to Section 4.4 on Competency Management).

For further guidance in preparing the organization's project management methodology, see Section 5 on Developing a Tailored Organizational Project Management Methodology.

4

4.2.2 Foundational Organizational Project Management Methodology

Foundational project management methodology is appropriate for organizations that are implementing procedures for their projects for the first time. The primary focus of foundational project management methodology is:

- Project level methodology, and

- Portfolio view of projects.

4.2.2.1 Project Management Implementation

The fundamentals at the project level are based upon the *PMBOK® Guide* Process Groups, which are typically performed in each project and are highly interactive.

In addition, the organization needs to add specific methodology steps or tasks that are directly aligned to the project types within the organization. These specific steps are used to tailor the methodology to fit the organization. The better the methodology aligns to the organization, the better the opportunities for project success and organizational adoption.

When planning and maintaining a project management methodology, it is important to consider the entire organization. Inclusion of cross-functional stakeholders who can contribute to the development of specific methodology steps is vital to ensure the integration of the business management framework into the project management methodology. These cross-functional stakeholders have knowledge of the requirements in their respective areas and offer detailed and unique perspectives, which are critical for tailoring a base methodology.

The following activities are useful for the development of a foundational project management methodology:

- **Establish an organizational definition of project management.** The definition should outline what project management is and what it is not. This definition will help to set expectations about project management results.

- **Establish an organizational definition of a project.** The definition should include minimum threshold characteristics such as cost, effort, risk, and/or duration. Initiatives that do not meet the minimum thresholds of the definition or are ongoing initiatives are not considered projects, and therefore, may be excluded from project management methodology requirements. However, it should be noted that these initiatives could benefit from the utilization of the project-level project management methodology, recognizing that tailoring for fit may be necessary.

In concert with the organizational definition of a project, the organization should consider the creation of a full lexicon of project management terms that will have meaning organization-wide. A full lexicon can provide a solid foundation for consistent communications to drive organizational clarity. The *PMI Lexicon of Project Management Terms* [8] contains frequently used project management terms with clear and concise definitions and may be used as a reference source.

- **Define and implement a project cataloging process to list all projects.** This cataloging process maintains high-level project information. Recommended information may include: project title, project manager, project sponsor(s), owning organization, project type. Process steps define the information needed to register a project, the exact mechanism used for registration (e.g., form, website), and how to submit the registration. This list is useful for leadership reviews of all project work within the organization. This activity eventually evolves into the portfolio view where all programs and projects are included in a single database or document for review and action.

- **Determine a set of project management processes that are appropriate for each project type.** Existing processes or procedures and successful programs and projects are a good source for template identification and development. It is generally recognized as good practice to reference the *PMBOK® Guide* – Fifth Edition, which details the project management processes that are aligned to the Process Groups and Knowledge Areas.

  Additionally, add specific methodology steps or tasks that are directly aligned to the project types within the organization, solicit input from cross-organization stakeholders, leverage existing organizational processes and procedures, use good practices from successful programs and projects, consider other industry standards, and review lessons learned.

- **Describe the selected project management processes using a consistent documentation structure and format.** Consistent documentation structure and format provides an expected level of content detail for each methodology step. Consider including a brief overview of the methodology and expected benefits along with a location for documentation archiving. Also, provide details for the methodology action steps such as:

  o *Description.* Provide a narrative description of what the methodology action is.

  o *Condition.* Describe the conditions required to permit execution of the action. For example, a methodology step supporting third-party management could have a condition of "use when third-party engagement is within scope." This is useful for methodology tailoring guidance.

  o *Inputs/outputs.* List the required and expected inputs and outputs by task.

  o *Roles.* Define the organizational roles that participate in an action. When several roles are involved, it is useful to describe the role engagement through consistent terms such as responsible, accountable, or informed. The roles and associated terms should also be defined within the organization's lexicon or glossary. Remember to include suppliers and other third-party groups as appropriate.

  o *Supporting assets/tools and techniques.* Identify supporting assets/tools and techniques, such as deliverable templates (blank templates created from best practice deliverables used on previous projects), reference materials (references to existing organizational processes/procedures), tools (existing organizational tools), training materials, or deliverable examples (populated best practice deliverables that provide an additional level of guidance by having a populated model to follow).

- **Outline a project-specific tailoring process to allow scalability and flexibility of the project management methodology.** Tailoring is designed to allow different types of projects to exclude processes that are not applicable. For example, if a project does not have any procurement requirements, the procurement processes are tailored out. The organization must also determine who will have the responsibility for tailoring. There are several approaches that can be taken to develop a tailoring process. Organizations may develop customized options or consider the following approaches:

  o *Project type models.* Pre-tailor standard methodology into project type packages. Select the appropriate methodology package for the project type; for example, global project, government project, internal project, or client contract project. This approach is useful for organizations that have project types that repeatedly execute in a similar fashion.

  o *Project size, complexity, and risk.* Pre-tailor standard methodology into project size/complexity/risk packages. Select the appropriate methodology package for the project size (e.g., small, intermediate, or large), or complexity and risk (e.g., internal or external, existing or new customer, known or new technology). This approach is useful for organizations that have differing methodology needs based on project size, complexity, and risk. An example of this is increased or decreased governance activities.

  o *Mandatory/tailor with condition.* Identify tasks that are mandatory or can be tailored. The tasks that can be tailored have a defined "condition." Condition describes what should exist for the action to be needed. Follow the guidance provided by the condition statements and ignore process steps that have conditions that do not apply. This approach is useful for organizations that have a variety of project types and characteristics where the maintenance of individual pre-tailored packages is unreasonable. This approach provides practitioner-aligned tailoring. Note: The methodology should contain mandatory tasks that are applicable regardless of project type. This provides a level of consistency for all projects.

  o *Tailoring questionnaire.* Develop a questionnaire for use during planning to capture the project type, size, and other characteristic information for the purpose of providing recommendations on methodology adjustments. This approach is similar to the mandatory/tailor with condition option and is useful for organizations that have a variety of project types and characteristics.

- **Establish project reporting models.** Develop requirements for different levels of management reporting. Include the development of processes to capture the required data at each level.

From an OPM perspective, organizational project management methodology is a tool used to engage and involve other parts of the business. Integrated business and project management processes and decisions are essential for effective OPM.

Table 4-1 provides guidance to help address alignment, fit, or project management methods when developing a methodology for a particular type of project. This list identifies topics that are covered by methodologies and

Table 4-1. Tailoring Considerations for Project Management Methods to Better Support OPM

Generic Project Life Cycle – *A Guide to the Project Management Body of Knowledge (PMBOK Guide®) – Fifth Edition*			
Starting the Project	**Organizing and Preparing**	**Carrying Out the Work**	**Closing the Project**
Specify participating internal stakeholder requirements and roles.	Engage enterprise risk management, financial, human resources, contracting, legal, internal audit, and other critical support services.	Ensure the engagement of contributing functions for support work as well as for technical work.	Define the phase and final closing points and associated activities with deliverables that are appropriate for the type of project.
Specify a project authorization method consistent with the organization's broader governance and management roles and responsibilities.	Ensure project management information system (PMIS) incorporates all stakeholders and their respective information systems appropriately.	Ensure stakeholder engagement that is appropriate for the role.	Define the documentation of and communication of results, success factors, and/or KPIs, in support of the business case, benefits realized, and lessons learned to specific stakeholders across the organization.
Link project charter to business case and current strategic objective(s).	Engage primary owners of resources in reconciling commitments to support the project.	Ensure communications with all appropriate stakeholders.	Integrate the summary of results into project performance database for each project type.
Identify program relationship, if any, as well as other dependencies.		Ensure decision events (stage gates) are mapped to appropriate portfolio/program context.	
Identify the portfolio to which the project should reside.		Define the level of monitoring and controlling, including the type of project change management process that best fits the type of project and organizational governance context.	
Prioritize the projects for decisions regarding resource assignment.		Define governance/sponsor roles and responsibilities involved in monitoring conformance to the charter and plan with attention to environmental changes and adherence to strategic alignment.	
Identify which established success factors/KPIs apply.		Identify a project change management process involving all key stakeholders and portfolio/program context.	
		Define internal and external audits for quality, financial, etc.	

provides important good practices to facilitate robust engagement across the organization. Organizations should tailor project management methodology that is consistent with the life cycle of a particular type of project. For further guidance in preparing the organization's project management methodology, see Section 5 (How to Develop a Tailored Organizational Project Management Methodology).

After the development of the methodology, consider the following to implement the methodology:

- **Update the organizational change management plan focusing on the people side of the change in addition to the process side.** Introducing new processes changes the way the work is done. Affected parties need to be coached on how to effectively adopt new practices. The benefits of new processes also need to be explained to gain buy-in from the users.

- **Update the training plan that identifies specific training needs for the different roles involved in the methodology.** Role-based training offers targeted training to the individual. Specific roles to be targeted are business leaders, project managers, PMO leaders, and project team members. Training topics include benefits of the methodology, how and when to use the methodology, tailoring guidance, tools training, and process compliance expectations. Refer to Section 4.4 (Competency Management).

- **Update the communications management plan to describe how, when, and by whom the methodology will be communicated to appropriate organization audiences.** The communications management plan is closely aligned to the change management plan and training plan, and should be executed with a full understanding of those components. The communications management plan may include: specific communication items (e.g., notice of decision, methodology announcement), communication media (e.g., newsletter, all employee meeting, email), targeted audience (e.g., project management community, organization-wide), communication requirements (e.g., mandatory, informational, storage guidelines), and frequency (e.g., one-time, monthly).

4.2.3 Improve Existing Organizational Project Management Methodology

Improved organizational project management methodology is appropriate for organizations that are successfully operating a project management methodology at the project level and are ready to advance their methodology into the project management disciplines of program management and/or portfolio management. Through the effective use of portfolio, program, and project management, organizations will possess the ability to employ reliable, established processes to meet their strategic objectives and obtain greater business value from project investments. All types of organizations should focus on attaining business value for their activities.

Using program management, organizations have the ability to align multiple projects for optimized or integrated costs, schedule, effort, and benefits. Program management focuses on project interdependencies and helps to determine the optimal approach for managing and realizing the desired benefits.

Portfolio management aligns multiple components (i.e., subportfolios, programs, projects, and related operations) to the organizational strategy, organized into portfolios or subportfolios, to optimize program or project objectives, dependencies, costs, timelines, benefits, resources, and risks. Using foundational project management methodology implementation at the project management level, a basic organizational portfolio is established. Additional subportfolios may be desired in the organization to more firmly position the program or project suite for success. For example, an organization may want to create subportfolios by functional area (e.g., finance, production, human resources) to more closely align programs and projects to the strategic objectives in those functions.

Program management and portfolio management are implemented into the project management methodology as needed by the organization (see Sections 4.2.3.1 and 4.2.3.2).

4.2.3.1 Program Management Implementation

Program management provides a framework for managing related efforts with consideration to key factors such as strategic benefits, coordinated planning, resourcing needs and availability, complex interdependencies, component integration, and optimized pacing. Essential program management responsibilities include planning the program, identifying and planning for benefits realization and sustainment, and identifying and controlling the interdependencies between projects. These responsibilities also include addressing escalated issues among the projects that comprise the program; and tracking the contribution of each project and the non-project work to the consolidated program benefits.

The integrative nature of program management processes involves coordinating the processes for each of the projects or program. This coordination applies across all program management activities and involves managing the processes at a level higher than that associated with individual projects. An example of this type of integration is the management of issues and risks needing resolution at the program level because they involve multiple projects or otherwise cross project boundaries, which cannot be addressed at the individual project level.

To plan and implement improved project management methodology with program management these activities should be completed:

- **Establish an organizational definition of a program.** The definition should include minimum threshold characteristics such as cost, effort, risk, and/or duration. Initiatives that do not meet the minimum thresholds of the definition may be excluded from methodology requirements.

- **Define and implement a program cataloging process that includes programs for the existing project list.** This cataloging process maintains high-level program information. Recommended information may include items such as program title, program manager, program sponsor(s), owning organization, and/or projects within the program. The process steps include the required information to register a program, the specific mechanism used to register information (e.g., form, website), and instructions on how to submit the registration.

- **Determine a set of program management processes that are appropriate to incorporate for each program type.** Refer to *The Standard for Program Management* – Third Edition, which details program-supporting processes aligned to the PMI program life cycle phases, generally recognized as good practice.

- **Describe the determined program management supporting processes using a consistent documentation structure and format.** Provide consistent documentation that describes the expected level of content and detail for each methodology step. Also, determine a central location for storing the documentation, for example, an existing website or shared directory for the organization's standards. Review the foundational project management methodology for suggested documentation of key elements.

- **Outline a program-specific tailoring process to allow scalability and flexibility of the project management methodology.** Tailoring allows different types of programs to tailor out processes that are not applicable. Review suggested foundational project management methodology for these approaches.

- **Update the existing OPM change management plan, training plan, and communications management plan to understand the new program management components.** Review suggested foundation project management methodology suggestions for these plans. Adjust for program management vs. project management.

For program management, when developing a methodology for a particular category or type of program, use Table 4-2 as a guide to help address alignment or fit within the organization. This is not an exhaustive list; however, it identifies important good practices to facilitate robust engagement across the organization. It is understood that organizations will tailor program management methodology to be consistent with the life cycle phases of a particular type of program. Refer to Section 5 (How to Develop a Tailored Project Management Methodology) for further guidance on tailoring.

4.2.3.2 Portfolio Management Implementation

Portfolio management is the centralized management of one or more portfolios that enables senior management to meet organizational goals and objectives through efficient decision making concerning one or more portfolios, programs, projects, and operations, as defined in *The Standard for Portfolio Management* – Third Edition.

Table 4-2. Tailoring Considerations for Program Management Methods to Better Support OPM

Program Life Cycle Phases [5]		
Program Definition Phase	**Program Benefits Delivery Phase**	**Program Closure Phase**
Establish a program authorization method consistent with the organization's broader governance and management roles and responsibilities.	Establish service level agreements (SLAs) with enterprise risk management, financial, human resources, contracting, legal, internal audit, and other critical support services.	Establish phase and final close points with associated activities and deliverables appropriate to type of program and its components.
Link program charter to business case and current strategic objectives.	Establish plan-driven stakeholder engagement appropriate to role.	Establish method to capture results/success factors/KPIs, support of business case, and benefits realized.
Establish dependencies, relationships, and priorities within and external to the program.	Ensure communications with all appropriate stakeholders.	Establish method to capture and communicate valuable lessons to specific stakeholders across the organization.
Identify and link to the portfolio in which the program and its components reside.	Establish decision events (stage gates) mapped to appropriate program and portfolio context.	Establish method to integrate summary results into program-project performance database for program type.
Establish priority of program for decisions regarding resource assignment within the program and within the host portfolio.	Establish the level of monitoring and controlling, including the type of change management process that best fits the type of program and organizational governance context.	
Establish participating internal stakeholders requirements and roles.		
Establish success factors, or KPIs, that apply to the program and its components.		
Engage primary owners of resources in reconciling priorities and commitments to support the program and its components.		
Establish governance/sponsor roles and responsibilities involved in monitoring conformance to business plan, charter, and program plan with attention to environmental changes and adherence to strategic alignment.		

Portfolio management ensures that interrelationships between programs and projects are identified and that resources (e.g., people, equipment, funding) are allocated, coordinated, and managed in accordance with organizational priorities. Portfolio management balances conflicting demands based on organizational priorities and capacity to achieve the benefits identified for successful performance of the portfolio.

Undertake the following activities when planning to implement improved project management methodology with portfolio management:

- **Define and implement a portfolio cataloging process that will add portfolio to the existing program/project list.** This cataloging process maintains high-level portfolio information. Recommended information may include items such as portfolio name, portfolio manager, owning organization, programs and projects within the portfolio, size, complexity, baseline budget, and milestones tailored to the organization's review preferences. The process steps include the information required to register a portfolio, the specific mechanism used to register information (e.g., form, website), and instructions on how to submit the registration.

- **Determine a set of portfolio management processes that are appropriate for each portfolio type.** Refer to *The Standard for Portfolio Management* – Third Edition, which details the portfolio processes that are generally recognized as good practice. This standard can be referenced for detailed information regarding each of these program-supporting processes.

- **Describe the identified portfolio management supporting processes into a consistent documentation structure and format.** Provide consistent documentation that describes the expected level of content and detail for each methodology step. Also, determine a central location for storing the documentation, for example, an existing website or shared directory for the organization's standards. Review the foundational project management methodology for suggested documentation of key elements.

- **Outline a portfolio-specific tailoring process to allow scalability and flexibility of the project management methodology.** Tailoring allows different types of portfolios to tailor out processes that are not applicable. Review foundational project management methodology suggestions for these approaches. Table 4-3 provides tailoring guidance for portfolio management methodology.

- **Update the existing organizational change management plan, training plan, and communications management plan to understand the new portfolio management components.** Review suggested foundation project management methodology for these plans. Adjust for portfolio management vs. project management.

For portfolio management, when developing a methodology for a particular portfolio, use Table 4-3 as a guide to help address alignment or fit within the organization. Table 4-3 identifies good practices to facilitate robust engagement across the organization. It is understood that organizations will tailor portfolio management methodology to be consistent with the Portfolio Management Process Groups.

4.2.4 Project Management Methodology KPIs

KPIs may be comprised of a varied set of metrics to be used to assess the effectiveness, influence, and maturity of the project management methodology and project performance. These are measurement objectives that are

Table 4-3. Tailoring Considerations for Portfolio Management Methods to Better Support OPM

Portfolio Management Process Groups - *The Standard for Portfolio Management* - Third Edition		
Defining Process Group	**Aligning Process Group**	**Authorizing and Controlling Process Group**
Establish the relationship of the portfolio plan to strategic activities within the organization and to current strategic objectives.	Ensure planned decision events (stage gates) are mapped to appropriate context and involve key stakeholders.	Establish an authorization method within and external to management of the portfolio consistent with the organization's broader governance and management roles, responsibilities, and delegation of authority.
Establish the relationship of portfolio operations and activities to existing business processes, structures, and operations.	Establish the level of monitoring and controlling, including the type of portfolio content change management process that best fits the portfolio and organizational governance context.	Establish governance/sponsor roles and responsibilities involved in monitoring conformance to charter and plan with attention to environmental changes and adherence to strategic alignment.
Establish participating internal stakeholder requirements and roles.	Establish a strategic change management process appropriate for portfolio context.	
Establish executive-approved success factors, or KPIs, to the aggregate portfolio and its components to ensure integration and consistency.	Establish a system for aggregating resource center information and activity throughout the organization.	Establish phase end/start requirements with key stakeholders for deliverables appropriate to type of program and its components.
Establish decision and communication flows with PMIS, financial, human resources, contracting, and other critical information systems appropriately.		Establish method to capture results/success factors/KPIs, support of business case, and benefits realized.
Establish working relationships with enterprise risk management and strategy management units.		Establish method to capture and communicate valuable lessons to specific stakeholders across the organization.
Engage primary owners of resources in reconciling priorities and commitments to support the portfolio and its components.		Establish method to integrate summary results into program-project performance database for program type.
Establish authority of portfolio manager to invoke decisions regarding components and priorities.		

derived from identified information needs and objectives and should be reviewed with leadership on a regular basis. Consider a KPI dashboard as a way to present KPI data to stakeholders. Examples of KPIs include:

- **Business Value and Benefits realization.** Business value and benefits realization planning drills down on the expected benefits for a given portfolio, program, or project, and details how each will be measured, who will measure them, and when they are measured. Planning accomplishes the following:

  o Helps to ensure that the business value and benefits of a given portfolio, program, or project are clearly defined for the stakeholders;

  o Documents benefits in such a way that they can be easily measured and evaluated during the course of the life cycle;

  o Allows the governing bodies to evaluate the expected net benefits to prioritize efforts;

  o Provides a strong reason to keep stakeholders and sponsors interested in supporting OPM; and

      ○ Develops business value and benefits realization KPIs (e.g., business process productivity increase percent, the actual increase in business productivity after the project management methodology has been tailored, expressed as a percentage; and cycle time reduction percent, the decrease in cycle time of a project that occurred after the project management methodology has been tailored, expressed as a percentage.)

- **On-time and on-budget delivery.** Examples include evaluation of expected and actual due dates for milestones and deliverables; expected and actual budget attainment; earned value indicators such as schedule performance index (SPI), cost performance index (CPI); deviation of planned hours of work; cost of managing processes; percentage of milestones missed; and percentage of overdue project tasks. Corresponding target performance levels are useful for analyzing the results, for example, a performance target of "90% of milestones are attained on-time."

- **Formal and informal quality audit results.** Examples include evaluation of deliverable defects and test results; percentage of rework attributable to ambiguous, inaccurate, or missing requirements; project team satisfaction index; project stakeholder satisfaction index; and percentage of requirements tested.

- **Lessons learned.** Capturing specific lessons learned helps management to make informed decisions when prioritizing future similar components.

- **Methodology compliance.** Assessment of methodology compliance covers the portfolio, program, or project.

- **Organizational Business Goals.** Assessment of organizational business goals.

4.3 Governance

OPM governance enables organizations to consistently manage projects and maximize the value of project outcomes. It provides a framework in which organizations can make decisions that satisfy business needs and expectations. OPM governance is achieved through the actions of a review and decision-making body that is charged with endorsing or approving recommendations for the organizational project management components under its authority, to include existing portfolio review boards. Consistent with organizational governance, OPM governance practices promote adherence to OPM policy throughout the organization. OPM governance varies based on the business needs of the organization.

Governance includes all levels of the organization and may transcend business lines. Governance is not limited to project management leadership, but includes representation from any business unit that has impact, influence, or involvement in portfolios, programs, and projects. It provides leadership involvement and support to the performing organization.

Effective OPM governance supports organizational success by:

- Establishing clear, well-understood agreements as to how the sponsoring organization will oversee, contribute, and support or align portfolios, programs, and projects; and conversely, the degree of autonomy that each will be given in the pursuit of its goals;

- Ensuring that the goals of the portfolios, programs, and projects remain aligned with the strategic vision, operational capabilities, and resource commitments of the organization;

- Establishing a set of robust KPIs that provides the ability to monitor and review the performance of the organization so as to base sound decisions upon; and

- Establishing regular performance reviews using a centralized venue to ensure alignment of the organizational strategy and to ensure that the organization is delivering the expected benefits, which includes a maturity assessment using a model such as *OPM3®*.

OPM governance supports the strategic alignment process that ensures that the portfolios, programs, and projects are appropriately aligned to the organizational goals and strategies. Then, business and project functions need to focus on the same goals to crystallize OPM benefits.

Other core-enabling processes implemented by the organization are integrated with governance through the review and monitoring of process-specific key performance indicators. Recommendations and initiatives are reviewed and accepted using the governance processes, which enhance current processes and methodologies identified during routine assessment and reviews.

4.3.1 How to Plan and Implement Governance

Planning and implementing OPM governance consists of identifying organizational-specific inputs based on an initial assessment of the organization's readiness for OPM.

The inputs of this activity include:

- Prior organizational assessments, including work culture assessments;

- Strategic alignment process details;

- Organizational risk tolerance;

- Understanding of existing management teams or governance boards within the organization; and

- Key performance indicators.

The outputs of this activity include (and note that some elements of these may already exist):

- OPM governance charter;

- OPM governance process and owner;

- Strategic alignment through portfolio, program, and project approval processes;

- Communications management plan; and

- Key performance indicators revised.

4.3.2 Foundational OPM Governance

Foundational OPM governance is appropriate for organizations who wish to expand or initiate project management methodologies across all organizational units involved in projects to ensure alignment with the strategic goals. Foundational OPM governance leverages an existing management team or governance board within the organization to assume the additional scope of OPM governance. Additional staff can be added as needed. This approach maintains an appropriate alignment of governance leadership with the core-enabling processes. OPM governance responsibilities include the following:

- Determine the most closely aligned manager, management team, or existing governance board. Make contact with the board leadership and secure agreement on additional OPM responsibilities.
- Establish roles and responsibilities for the governance board and its members.
- Develop a communications management plan that describes the governance board function, including its purpose, objectives, attendance, frequency, and meeting content.
- Document and finalize the charter, scope, and membership of the governance board, including how they will be integrated with the portfolio, program, or project approval process.
- Review and implement the strategic alignment process.
- Establish and approve the appropriate KPIs.

4.3.3 Improved OPM Governance

Improved OPM governance is appropriate for organizations that have an established OPM governance function, similar to what is described in Section 4.3.2. As the OPM function expands, improved governance is required to support the ultimate goal of being enterprise wide as follows:

- Incorporate additional members to the governance board to represent all of the OPM-enabled business units within the enterprise that work in concert to accomplish the organizational strategy.
- Determine whether a budget is needed for the governance function. Pursue budget approval as appropriate.
- Institutionalize the OPM governance process by updating the charter to include applicable changes in scope and membership.
- Transform the performance of the organization through regular KPI reviews and assessments.
- Identify, prioritize, and execute continuous improvement initiatives.

4.3.4 Key Performance Indicators for OPM Governance

Various key performance indicators are used to assess the OPM governance function. Examples of KPIs include number of program or project approvals, percentage of programs or projects that complete project tollgates or project phases in a timely manner, number of continuous improvement or corrective action initiatives identified, and annual volume of project delays outside acceptable thresholds.

4.4 Competency Management

OPM competency management facilitates the timely and appropriate assessment of the skills and development of the experience necessary to implement portfolios, programs, and projects within an organization. Competency management transcends the organization and is not limited to those competencies necessary to manage a project. For this reason, the OPM processes for competency management should be conducted in concert with the human resources organization. Competency management ensures that all levels, including process owners, functional managers, and executives, have the competencies necessary to successfully deliver the portfolio, programs, and projects and understand their roles in the process.

Competency management encompasses assessing the skills and capabilities needed for managing projects and programs within a portfolio; assessing the organization's available resources necessary to meet those needs; providing the training to develop the required skills and capabilities, along with informing all parties of their respective roles; forecasting long-term competency needs and developing a strategy to meet them; and ensuring continuous learning and improvement. As with all OPM processes, competency management should be tailored for the organization and take into consideration the organization's structure including roles and responsibilities as well as the organization's strategy and purpose. PMI's *Project Manager Competency Development Framework (PMCDF)* [9] can be used as a resource.

OPM competency management supports the strategic alignment, governance, and project management methodology processes by: (a) ensuring near-term and long-term planning for competency needs; (b) ensuring everyone in the organization understands their roles and responsibilities relative to delivering portfolios, programs, and projects; (c) ensuring everyone in the organization has the associated skills and knowledge, and has an opportunity to expand that knowledge; and (d) providing mechanisms for continuous improvement and learning.

While the focus of this section is on specific competencies supporting program and project delivery within an OPM context, organizations should understand the need to foster improvement of the soft skills, particularly communication and leadership. This is especially important when integrating dissimilar project management and business management units within an organization into an OPM framework.

4.4.1 How to Plan and Implement OPM Competency Management

When an organization understands OPM maturity and has identified their target organizational maturity, they can make informed choices to ensure a robust competency management infrastructure.

The inputs for OPM competency management include:

- List of portfolios, programs, and projects;
- Project skills assessment (to identify skills needed to deliver a specific project);
- Skills and experience assessment of existing portfolio, program, and project managers;
- Organizational skills assessment (to understand whether the skills needed can be provided for within an organization or not); and
- Organizational structure (to identify sources for the skills within the organization).

The outputs for OPM competency management include (some elements may already exist):

- Updated skills assessments,
- Understanding of which organization will provide the needed skills,

- Identification of external sources for skills that are not available within the organization,

- Competency model (for improved implementation),

- Career development framework (for improved implementation),

- Training curriculum (for improved implementation),

- Knowledge management system (for improved implementation), and

- KPIs.

4.4.2 Foundational OPM Competency Management

At a minimum, an organization needs to understand the portfolio structure (e.g., the projects and programs that support the organization's strategic plan or business case), the organizational structure, and the skills and abilities of the workforce (including where to acquire resources if not available within the organization). In a foundational organization, the skills and capabilities needed to deliver the portfolio, programs, and projects may be sourced from various locations (e.g., project team, technical team, information technology office, human resources, procurement, financial resources, external suppliers, etc.). The goal for competency management within a basic OPM implementation is to ensure that the required skills and capabilities are available in order to deliver the project. The steps for a basic implementation are as follows:

- Review the list of programs and projects that are necessary to deliver the organization's strategy. If the organization does not have a list, consult PMI standards to assist the organization with organizing their work into programs and projects [5, 6].

- Assess skills necessary to deliver the projects. The *PMBOK® Guide* – Fifth Edition, the *PMI Project Manager Competency Development Framework (PMCDF)* and other project management standards provide an overview of the processes that should be performed when managing a project. PMI's PathPro® for Organizations is an available assessment tool. These functions include but are not limited to: project management, resource management (i.e., financial, human, materials, and facilities, etc.), contract management, schedule management, risk management, and quality management.

- Perform a skills gap analysis. Review the organizational structure to determine whether the needed skills are available within the organization or whether they will need to be procured.

- Identify sources for developing needed skills. This may include the use of existing experts within the organization to mentor and train others, and the development or procurement of training to build the needed skills. Organizations should be prepared to acquire skilled resources from other sources when they are not available internally.

- Reassess the skills and competency requirements needed to deliver the business case for OPM, as needed. Consider changes in organizational structure, as well as changes in the organization's strategy and portfolio, including additions and deletions to the program and project structure. Periodically assess and align the skill set of the organization's workforce. As an organization evolves, it is expected that the cadre of experienced workforce will grow, but this growth is not always proportional to the evolution of programs and projects.

- Understand how hiring and attrition impact the organization's capabilities, keeping in mind that skills can be developed, transferred from experienced personnel, or procured from outside of the organization.

4.4.3 Improved OPM Competency Management

For an improved OPM implementation, competency management will enhance capabilities incrementally, with a desired end goal of having a comprehensive infrastructure for competency management. An organization that is improving their competency management process should incrementally expand their processes until the desired state is reached. The implementation process should take into consideration constraints such as funding and existing career path structures. It is common for the competency management system to evolve as an organization becomes more mature and when OPM is embedded into the organizational culture.

In a fully enhanced or mature OPM implementation, program and project management is integral to the business model, an infrastructure is in place, the roles and responsibilities are well understood, and the need for OPM is no longer debated. The attributes of competency management within an advanced OPM organization include: (a) a competency model; (b) a career development framework; (c) a training curriculum; (d) developmental opportunities (including mentoring and internships as well as on-the-job training); (e) knowledge-sharing services; and (f) organizational support. Although not appropriate for all organizations, a mature organization will also consider the value of implementing certification programs to ensure the workforce has achieved a certain quality standard: project management, acquisition, financial, and quality certifications etc. The activities for implementing improved OPM competency management include the following:

- Develop and implement a competency model that is newly created or adapted from another organization. This model typically includes multiple levels such as novice, mid-career, and expert.

- Develop and implement a career development framework that provides a path for an individual to progressively develop necessary skills. Learning strategies for each level include a combination of training classes and developmental opportunities.

- Develop and implement a training curriculum benchmarked against similar organizations at an advanced OPM level to determine the best solution for the organization. Training should be developed to address the entire skill set and also should be provided to the leadership and support functions.

- Identify experiential learning and developmental opportunities that are targeted and more structured than classroom and on-the-job development experiences, for example, formal mentoring processes, pilot projects, and formal development programs.

- Implement an infrastructure of knowledge sharing, communities of practice, and lessons learned to propagate good practices across the organization and with the organization's stakeholders and partners.

- Provide organizational support to responsible groups in addition to all supporting organizational elements and staff to convey how they are expected to contribute to the delivery of strategy through OPM and to ensure they have the skills and capabilities necessary to do so.

- Assess alignment of the organization's competency needs and infrastructure, strategy, organizational structure, existing skill set, and programmatic demographics, all of which evolve over time, to ensure that the needed skills are available to support the organization's long-term objectives.

- Reevaluate the assessment questionnaire referred to in Appendix X3 along with the KPIs and metrics to determine whether the organization is performing at its desired level.

- Benchmark against other organizations with similar business models to identify good practices.

4.4.4 KPIs for OPM Competency Management

A variety of KPIs are used to assess an organization's competency management implementation within the OPM framework. At the organizational level, establish KPIs to ensure that program and project teams have the skills necessary to deliver the program or project and that long-range competency needs are met. Sample KPIs include: number of courses offered, number of people trained, resources available vs. project and program needs, the number of certified project managers (for example, Project Management Professional (PMP)®, Certified Associate in Project Management (CAPM)®, Program Management Professional (PgMP)®), the number of communities of practice coupled with level of activity within a community of practice, and the measurement of project management performance for different levels of skills, knowledge, and experience.

4.5 Summary

Highlights from each section describing the four core-enabling processes, which are essential to the delivery of an organization's strategic objectives, are as follows:

4.5.1 Strategic Alignment

- Strategic alignment, when supported by governance, enables an organization to consistently manage and align portfolios with business strategy to maximize value of outcomes.

- Organizations should align portfolios, along with responsible organizational elements and available capital resources, to a documented strategic plan.

- Preferably, the alignment of portfolios, responsible organizational elements, and available capital resources are accomplished prior to formal initiation.

- Alignment of portfolios, responsible organizational elements, and available capital resources are managed and updated with changes to the organization's strategic plan.

4.5.2 Organizational Project Management Methodology

- Project management methodology is a critical component of OPM because of the organizational integration with an effective project management methodology.

- Project management methodology encompasses portfolios, programs, and projects.

- Project management methodology tailoring is based upon the requirements and needs of organizational stakeholders and should accommodate different types of portfolios, programs, and projects.

- Organizations that use standardized project management practices have significantly more projects that meet their original goals and business intent, and finish within budget and on time.

4.5.3 Governance

- The OPM governance function needs to be owned by a defined body that has clear roles and responsibilities.
- An OPM governance charter that defines the OPM scope, membership, and process should be documented and approved.
- As OPM function expands, the governance board should represent all relevant business units within the enterprise.
- OPM governance implies adherence to OPM policy and continuous improvement.

4.5.4 Competency Management

- Systematic forecasting and planning is essential for the development and retention of current and future competencies that are necessary to deliver the organization's strategy through OPM.
- Sound competency management typically includes a competency model, a career development framework, formal and informal training programs, and mechanisms to promote continuous improvement.
- Competencies should be developed and nurtured within all groups responsible for delivering programs and projects so that everyone understands how they contribute to delivery of the strategy through OPM.
- Organization should have a tailored approach to developing and maintaining necessary competencies to reflect the unique aspects of the organization.

5

HOW TO DEVELOP A TAILORED ORGANIZATIONAL PROJECT MANAGEMENT METHODOLOGY

5.1 Introduction

Organizational project management methodology is a system of practices, techniques, procedures, and rules used by those who perform portfolio, program, and project work to meet requirements and deliver benefits. This methodology covers all levels and facets of performing projects, regardless of form, in an organization. It is the heart of the OPM concept because it connects critical parts of the organization. The other core-enabling processes facilitate putting the right project management methodology in place. An effectively tailored methodology makes appropriate and useful connections and modifications with the business model of the organization. The result is a tailored project management methodology with the flexibility to adjust to future needs and changes within the organization.

All organizations are unique as demonstrated by their different objectives, cultures, business models, values, organizational models, strategic drivers, processes and procedures, and internal and external constraints (e.g., regulations). Even organizations that share a common business sector implement their strategies differently. Organizational project management methodology works best when it is tailored for effective use within the context of an organization and is aligned to the needs of the business. The methodology is customized and applied to portfolios, programs, and projects based on the needs and experience of the organization and project. Methodology application or fit varies by organization depending upon the characteristics of the programs and projects it performs.

In this section, the example of developing a tailored methodology applies to projects only. Characteristics such as project type, size, and complexity are basic considerations. The following examples demonstrate how these characteristics modify the manner in which the project methodology is applied:

- An IT project requires technical testing with other system components. The methodology supports integration activities, stakeholders, and processes.

- A facilities project requires the coordination of third-party products and services. The methodology supports third-party management guidance and processes.

- A highly complex project requires enhanced monitoring and control methods to ensure tight alignment of all elements. Tailoring of the monitoring and control practices for the required enhanced scrutiny is applicable.

When an organization manages a number of unique types of projects, it should consider developing multiple methodologies. Multiple methodologies provide consistency within the project type and allow the organization to realize the benefits referenced in the Pulse of the Profession™ study [2]. Examples of different types of projects that may require different methodologies include, but are not limited to, construction, software, aerospace, and pharmaceutical projects.

Project management methodology utilizes existing organizational process assets to provide organization-specific structure and guidance, which improves the success of project completion. These organizational process assets include policies, procedures, and knowledge bases (such as lessons learned and historical performance information) specific to and used by the performing organization. Additional organizational process assets may include completed project schedules, risk data, earned value data, benefits realization of programs, and aggregated risk management effectiveness of portfolio management. Organizational process assets are inputs to most planning processes and should be integrated in the project management methodology. Project management methodology is a critical component of OPM methodology and should contain specific references and call-outs to these organizational process assets rather than recreating or excluding them. For example:

- Human resource management activities should reference organizational human resource policies.
- Cost management activities should reference organizational financial controls procedures (e.g., time reporting, required expenditure and disbursement reviews, accounting codes, and standard contract provisions).
- The use of organization-specific templates or forms (e.g., risk register, work breakdown structure, project schedule network diagram, and contract templates) is expected as part of the project management methodology. It may be necessary to revise and supplement existing organizational process assets as OPM implementation matures.

5.2 Developing the Methodology

The following process assists an organization in tailoring its project management methodology, which can be used with minor modifications to develop portfolio and program methodologies. Organizations should consider developing a unique methodology for each project type. If there are similarities in the project types, organizations may consider modifying existing project management methodologies to simplify the methodology development process. Regardless of whether an organization is developing its first methodology or expanding upon an existing set of methodologies, these process steps should be followed to ensure no unique aspects of the project type are overlooked.

The simple inputs, constraints, outputs, and resources (ICOR) diagram shown in Figure 5-1 depicts a high-level process that may be used to generate a tailored methodology.

There are several approaches that can be taken to develop a tailoring process. Organizations can consider the following approach described in Sections 5.3 through 5.11 or create their own.

5.3 Identify Types of Projects

Every organization is unique and needs to determine how to distinguish between project types. To distinguish among project types, organizations can ask the following questions:

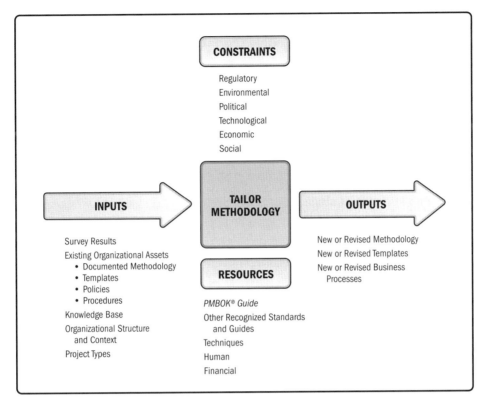

Figure 5-1. Methodology Tailoring Process

- Are there common lines of business (e.g., construction, aerospace, pharmaceutical) that deliver similar projects?

- Are there common levels of risk associated with the project?

- Are there varying levels of complexity (e.g., widgets developed in a single location with stable industrial bases vs. international efforts with multiple components that are required to be integrated in order to deliver the project)?

- Are there internal and/or external customers?

- What is the variance in size of the types of projects performed?

- What is the duration of the project?

- What is the urgency?

- Will the project have significant public or media attention?

- Are the project deliverables well-defined or unknown (e.g., building a bridge vs. performing research to test a theory)?

- Are the technologies necessary to deliver the project to maturity or do they need to be developed (e.g., building a conventional combustion engine or the next generation of technology for transportation)?

- Is the project labor or capital intensive, or both?

- Are there any regulatory agencies that need to be involved or regulations that must be met?

5.4 Identify Inputs

Identify the inputs to the project management methodology. There are many considerations when tailoring a methodology to a project type, which include the following:

- **Results of organizational survey.** Described in Section 3.1 and Appendix X3 of this practice guide.

- **Enterprise environmental factors.** Described in Section 2.1.5 of the *PMBOK® Guide* – Fifth Edition. Think "enterprise-wide" when planning and maintaining the project management methodology. Include cross-organization stakeholders (including, but not limited to, human resources, finance, legal, information systems/technology, training, etc.) who can contribute to the development of specific methodology steps or tasks. This is vital to ensure the integration of the business management framework into the project management methodology to achieve the organization's strategic goals and objectives. These cross-organization stakeholders bring the collective knowledge of their areas or business units and offer the detailed and unique perspective that is critical for tailoring a base methodology. Without the addition of the unique characteristics of the organization and its areas/business units, the organization may find little value in the methodology and fall short in its attempt to develop and implement OPM.

- **Organizational process assets.** Described in Section 2.1.4 of the *PMBOK® Guide* – Fifth Edition. Project management methodology utilizes existing organizational process assets to provide organization-specific structure and guidance, which improves the success of project completion. These organizational process assets include policies, procedures, and knowledge bases (e.g., lessons learned and historical performance information), specific to and used by the performing organization. Organizational process assets may include completed project schedules, risk data, earned value data, benefits realization of programs, and aggregated risk management effectiveness of the portfolio. Organizational process assets are inputs to most planning processes and should be integrated within the project management methodology. Since project management methodology is a critical part of OPM methodology, the organizational process assets should be referred to rather than recreated or excluded. For example, human resource management activities should reference organizational human resource policies; cost management activities should specify organizational financial controls procedures (e.g., time reporting, required expenditure and disbursement reviews, accounting codes, and standard contract provisions).

- **Existing templates.** Templates or forms are part of the project management methodology (e.g., risk register, work breakdown structure, project schedule network diagram, and contract templates).

- **Organizational structure.** Organizational structure (e.g., hierarchical, matrix, etc.) and culture (e.g., efficiency-focused, risk-focused, customer-focused, etc.) should shape the development of the methodology and corporate culture.

- **Organizational context or environment.** Organizational context and environment should also be considered. Examples include:

  o Regulated environment,

  o Government agency or nongovernment organization,

  o Predictive approach vs. iterative/incremental (agile),

  o International, regional, or local market,

  o Developing economy/market,

  o Internal vs. external customers,

  o Timing of capital infusion (early or late),

  o New product development, and

  o Tangible vs. intangible end product.

5.5 Identify Constraints

Identify the constraints to the project types. Constraints are those items that are required to be followed without exception. Examples include regulations and laws including environmental, reporting, or safety.

5.6 Identify Resources

Identify the resources available to assist with the development of the methodology.

- Identify any existing project management methodologies that can be modified to support additional project types. Leveraging existing methodologies may be beneficial depending on the magnitude of difference between project types. Organizations should characterize the differences and ensure those differences are considered when using an existing methodology as a basis for a new project methodology.

- Identify relevant published guidance found in the *PMBOK® Guide,* other PMI standards, other publications, templates, or existing methodologies. These standards and other documents can provide foundational guidance that may be customized to fit the specific requirements of the organization and its projects based on the other input.

5.7 Develop and Document the Methodology

When developing a tailored methodology, ensure that the action plan considers the inputs, constraints, and resources. Each organization should have a procedure for developing and documenting methodology (indicated by the center box in the ICOR diagram shown in Figure 5-1). The following is an example of a process to develop a methodology:

- Assemble a multidisciplinary team that includes representation from key stakeholder functions in the organization that will be responsible for developing, supporting, and executing organizational project management processes.

- Lay out the life cycle for the type of project.

- Map out the steps needed for each phase of the life cycle. A flowchart that includes responsibilities is recommended.

- Identify the business areas that are affected by each of the steps in the life cycle.

- Determine any modifications needed to the existing business or project processes. If it is a new process, begin with the documented current state.

- Review the Project Management Process Group Knowledge Area Mapping (see Table 3-1 of the *PMBOK® Guide – Fifth Edition*) and determine which processes are required for each phase. Consider other resources, as applicable.

- Document each of the *PMBOK® Guide – Fifth Edition* processes with regard to how they are tailored to fit within the organization's existing processes, standards, and requirements. Examples include:

  o *Development of a communications management plan.* The communications management plan for large organizations will need to be more formal than small organizations. In a regulated environment, reporting to government agencies may be required.

  o *Development of the procurement management plan.* Determine whether the entire project will be developed in-house or whether contracted services will be utilized.

  o *Development of the scope management plan.* Document how the scope of the project will be defined, validated, and controlled.

  o *Development of stakeholder management plan.* Develop the appropriate strategies to manage and engage the stakeholders throughout the project life cycle.

- Create any required templates or checklists that document the necessary steps for the organization and corresponding industry.

- Document the methodology. This is the organization's tailored methodology based on the *PMBOK® Guide. – Fifth Edition.* Be sure to consider the level of flexibility (i.e., mandatory or nonmandatory?) for each process step.

5.8 Derive Output

The output of this process is the documented, tailored methodology ready for application to the project type identified.

5.9 Conduct Continuous Improvement

Organizations evolve and environmental factors change. It is important to periodically reassess and update this methodology.

5.10 Monitor Key Performance Indicators

Key performance indicators may be comprised of a varied set of metrics to assess the effectiveness, influence, and maturity of the project management methodology. See Section 4 for examples of KPIs used in project management methodology.

5.11 Repeat for Each of the Different Types of Projects

Repeat these steps (Sections 5.4 through 5.11) for all of the different project types using the first one as a basis for the others.

5.12 Summary

5.12.1 Developing a Tailored Project Management Methodology

- Identify the inputs that the organization gathered during the assessment phase. These include any current practices, methodologies, and processes that you may already have.
- Identify any constraints that the organization is required to operate under whether required or agreed upon.
- Document the organization's types of projects; if only one type is identified, make sure the methodology is scalable to the size, complexity, risk, and other factors the organization chooses.

APPENDIX X1
CONTRIBUTORS AND REVIEWERS OF *IMPLEMENTING ORGANIZATIONAL PROJECT MANAGEMENT: A PRACTICE GUIDE*

X1.1 Core Committee

The following individuals were members of the Core Committee responsible for drafting the practice guide, including review and adjudication of reviewer recommendations.

Paul E. Shaltry, MA, PMP, Committee Chair
Sandy H. Cobb, PgMP, PMP, Committee Vice Chair
Michael C. Collins, PMP
Colette Connor, PMP
Melvin G. Frank, PMP
Felicia E. Hong, MBA, PMP
Conrado Morlan, PgMP, PMP
Norman K. Prevost, PMP
Terry Lee Ricci, PgMP, PMP
Gary J. Sikma, PMP
Sandra E. Smalley
Karl F. Best, CAPM, CStd, Standards Project Specialist

X1.2 Review Team

The following individuals were members of the review team responsible for review of the practice guide.

Terry Lee Ricci, PgMP, PMP, Review Team Lead
Hagit Landman, PMP, PMI-SP
M. Aslam Mirza, MBA, PMP

Andrea G. Demaria, PMP, MSP
Mercedes Martinez Sanz, PMP
Daud Nasir, PMP, LSSBB

X1.3 Subject Matter Expert Reviewers

The following individuals were invited subject matter experts who reviewed the draft and provided recommendations through the SME review.

Ayman Atallah, PMP

Claudia M. Baca, PMP, OPM3 Certified Professional

Maria Cristina Barbero, PMP, PMI-ACP

Parthasarathy Bhaumik, MBA, PMP

Marty Biggs, PMP

Dennis L. Bolles, PMP

Larry Bull

Steve Butler

Joel Crook, MSBA, PgMP

Michele L. Deo, MBA, PMP

Paul C. Dinsmore, PMP, PMI Fellow

Wayne D. Ellis, PE, PMP

Claude Emond

Chris Field, MBCS, PMP

Brian Grafsgaard, PgMP, PMP

Leslie A. Griffin, PMP

Ruth Anne Guerrero, MBA, PMP

Salah M. Haswah, MBA, PMP

Anca Ivanov, PMP

Kris Jennes, MSC, PMP

Sally E. Johnston, MA, PMP

Sahin Kaya, MSc, PMP

Scott Kirkland

Hava Kurt, MBA, CSM

Hagit Landman, PMP, PMI-SP

Craig Letavec, PMP, PgMP

Ginger Levin, PhD, PgMP, PMP

Stacey M. López, PMP

Eduardo Luna Librero

Mercedes Martinez Sanz, PMP

Diane Miller

Vladimir Antonio Mininel, PMP

M. Aslam Mirza, MBA, PMP

Reka Mishra, PMP, ITILv3

Nathan Mourfield, MBA, PMP

Claudia Ivonne Munguia Mejia

Mordecai Muswera ACMA, PMP

Shashank Neppalli

Gert Noordzij, MBA, FIAQ

Daniel G. O'Sheedy, PhD, PMP

Beth Ouellette, PgMP, PMP

Yvan Petit, PhD, PMP

Rogerio de Mello Pires, PMP

Piyush Prakash, PMP, Prince2

Jobst Scheuermann

Tim Schmeising-Barnes

Gery Schneider

Alana Schock, MEd, PMP

Jen L. Skrabak, MBA, PMP

Joe Sopko

Suhaib Taqvi

Lawrence Tobin, MS, PMP

Valerie van der Klis, PMP

X1.4 PMI Standards Member Advisory Group (MAG)

The following individuals are members of the PMI Standards Member Advisory Group, who provided direction to and final approval for the practice guide.

Monique Aubry, PhD, MPM

Margareth Fabiola dos Santos Carneiro, MSc, PMP

Larry Goldsmith, MBA, PMP

Cynthia Snyder, MBA, PMP

Chris Stevens, PhD

Dave Violette, MPM, PMP

John Zlockie, MBA, PMP, Standards Manager

X1.5 PMI Production Staff

Donn Greenberg, Manager, Publications
Roberta Storer, Product Editor
Barbara Walsh, Publications Production Supervisor

APPENDIX X2
AN OVERVIEW OF *OPM3®* ORGANIZATIONAL ENABLERS AND MAPPING TO THIS PRACTICE GUIDE

OPM advances organizational capability by linking portfolio, program, and project management principles and practices with organizational enablers (e.g., structural, cultural, technological, and human resource practices) to support strategic goals. An organization measures its capabilities, then plans and implements improvements toward the systematic achievement of best practices. As elaborated on in more detail in *OPM3®*, the four categories of organizational enablers are summarized as follows:

- **Structural** (S):
    - Drive reporting relationships among employees, allocation of resources, and alignment to strategy.
    - Establish strategic alignment and resource allocation based on organizational structures.

- **Cultural** (C):
    - Embrace portfolio, program, and project management.
    - Establish governance, policy, and vision.
    - Act as sponsors rather than administrators.
    - Support communities where OPM best practices can be shared and leveraged.

- **Technological** (T):
    - Perform manual tasks better, faster, and cheaper.
    - Encourage the reuse of good practices and techniques.
    - Improve knowledge sharing.
    - Invest in management systems that support effective portfolio, program, and project management.
    - Share practices and techniques across projects.
    - Develop a methodology that becomes the standard for the performance of programs and projects.
    - Benchmark portfolio, program, and project performance against comparable organizations.

- **Human Resource** (HR):
    - Have the right people in place to execute the necessary roles.
    - Ensure successful application of OPM and higher organizational performance using competency management, individual performance appraisals, and training investments.

Table X2-1 cross references the eighteen organizational enablers listed in *OPM3®* by category (structural, cultural, technological, or human resource), and then maps each organizational enabler to the section in this practice guide with relevant information or a specific component or practice that is required to accomplish implementation and/or improvement of OPM. Refer to *OPM3®* for a more detailed explanation of how the 18 organizational enablers are used in the *OPM3®* maturity model.

Table X2-1. Cross Mapping of *OPM3®* Organization Enablers to Practice Guide Sections

OPM3® Organizational Enablers (Category)	OPM Practice Guide Topic Section Reference
Benchmarking (T)	OPM Essentials for Implementation (Section 1.4) Continuous Improvement (Section 2.1.1.2) Develop Implementation Plan (Section 3.3.1) How to Plan and Implement Strategic Alignment (Section 4.1.1)
Competency Management (HR)	OPM Essentials for Implementation (Section 1.4) Identify Future State (Section 3.1.2) Perform Gap Analysis (Section 3.1.3) Develop Implementation Plan (Section 3.3.1) Competency Management (Section 4.4) Recommended Survey Questions (Appendix X3)
Governance (C)	OPM Essentials for Implementation (Section 1.4) Evaluate Current Organizational State (Section 2.1.2.2) Identify Future State (Section 3.1.2) Perform Gap Analysis (Section 3.1.3) Develop Implementation Plan (Section 3.3.1) Continuous Improvement (Section 3.4) Strategic Alignment (Section 4.1) Organizational Project Management Methodology (Section 4.2) Governance (Section 4.3) Recommended Survey Questions (Appendix X3)
Individual Performance Appraisals (HR)	Improved OPM Competency Management (Section 4.4.3)
Knowledge Management and PMIS (T)	Portfolio Management Implementation (Section 4.2.3.2) How to Plan and Implement OPM Competency Management (Section 4.4.1) Recommended Survey Questions (Appendix X3)
Management Systems (T)	Recommended Survey Questions (Appendix X3)
Organizational Project Management Communities (C)	Recommended Survey Questions (Appendix X3)
Organizational Project Management Methodology (T)	OPM Essentials for Implementation (Section 1.4) Organizational Project Management Methodology (Section 4.2) Governance (Section 4.3) Competency Management (Section 4.4) How to Develop a Tailored Organizational Project Management Methodology (Section 5) Recommended Survey Questions (Appendix X3)
Organizational Project Management Policy and Vision (C)	Overview of OPM Basics (Section 1.1) Tailoring the Approach to Implementing OPM Core Processes in an Organization (Section 1.6) Step 3 – Propose the OPM Business Case (Section 2.1.3) Develop Implementation Plan (Section 3.3.1) Pilot and Implement OPM (Section 3.3.2)
Organizational Project Management Practices (T)	Introduction (Section 1) Overview of OPM Basics (Section 1.1) OPM Fit with the Organization's Business Model (Section 1.5) Tailoring the Approach to Implementing OPM Core Processes in an Organization (Section 1.6) Organizational Change Management (Section 2.1.1.3) Evaluate Current Organizational State (Section 2.1.2.2) Discovery and Analysis (Section 3.1) Implementation Roadmap (Section 3.2) Implementation (Section 3.3) Organizational Project Management Methodology (Section 4.2) How to Develop a Tailored Organizational Project Management Methodology (Section 5) Recommended Survey Questions (Appendix X3)

AS = structural; C = cultural; T = technological; HR = human resource.

Table X2-1. Cross Mapping of *OPM3®* Organization Enablers to Practice Guide Sections *(Continued)*

OPM3® Organizational Enablers (Category)	OPM Practice Guide Topic Section Reference
Organizational Project Management Techniques (T)	Tailoring the Approach to Implementing OPM Core Processes in an Organization (Section 1.6) Develop Implementation Plan (Section 3.3.1) Organizational Project Management Methodology (Section 4.2) How to Develop a Tailored Organizational Project Management Methodology (Section 5) Recommended Survey Questions (Appendix X3)
Organizational Structures (S)	Evaluate Current Organizational State (Section 2.1.2.2) Portfolio Management Implementation (Section 4.2.3.2) Improved OPM Competency Management (Section 4.4.3) Recommended Survey Questions (Appendix X3)
Project Management Metrics (T)	Continuous Improvement (Section 2.1.1.2) Perform Gap Analysis (Section 3.1.3) Identify and Prioritize Initiatives (Section 3.2.1) Develop Implementation Plan (Section 3.3.1) Realize Benefits (Section 3.3.3) Continuous Improvement (Section 3.4) Project Management Methodology Key Performance Indicators (KPIs) (Section 4.2.4) Improved OPM Competency Management (Section 4.4.3) How to Develop a Tailored Organizational Project Management Methodology (Section 5) Recommended Survey Questions (Appendix X3)
Project Management Training (HR)	OPM Fit with the Organization's Business Model (Section 1.5) Share OPM Information (Section 2.1.2.1) Evaluate Current Organizational State (Section 2.1.2.2) Develop Implementation Plan (Section 3.3.1) Pilot and Implement OPM (Section 3.3.2) How to Plan and Implement an Organizational Project Management Methodology (Section 4.2.1) Competency Management (Section 4.4) How to Develop a Tailored Organizational Project Management Methodology (Section 5) Recommended Survey Questions (Appendix X3)
Project Success Criteria (T)	Step 3 – Propose the OPM Business Case (Section 2.1.3) Develop Implementation Plan (Section 3.3.1) Recommended Survey Questions (Appendix X3)
Resource Allocation (S)	Introduction (Section 1) Develop Implementation Plan (Section 3.3.1) Realize Benefits (Section 3.3.3) How to Plan and Implement Strategic Alignment (Section 4.1.1) Project Management Implementation (Section 4.2.2.1) Governance (Section 4.3) How to Develop a Tailored Organizational Project Management Methodology (Section 5) Recommended Survey Questions (Appendix X3)
Sponsorship (C)	OPM Fit with the Organization's Business Model (Section 1.5) Sustained Leadership (Section 2.1.1.1) Next Steps – Form the OPM Implementation Team (Section 2.2) Recommended Survey Questions (Appendix X3)
Strategic Alignment (S)	OPM Essentials for Implementation (Section 1.4) Understand the Organization's Strategy and Project Management Practices (Section 3.1.1) Identify Future State (Section 3.1.2) Perform Gap Analysis (Section 3.1.3) Develop Implementation Plan (Section 3.3.1) Strategic Alignment (Section 4.1) Project Management Implementation (Section 4.2.2.1) How to Plan and Implement Governance (Section 4.3.1) Competency Management (Section 4.4) Recommended Survey Questions (Appendix X3)

AS = structural; C = cultural; T = technological; HR = human resource.

APPENDIX X3
RECOMMENDED SURVEY QUESTIONS REGARDING IMPLEMENTATION OF OPM INITIATIVES

The questions below are intended to help an organization perform a self-assessment to determine where it stands relative to important implementation factors related to OPM. This survey is designed for organizations in the foundational or improvement stages. It is not intended to be an exhaustive or restrictive list but rather guide users to typical critical implementation considerations. Another approach would be to conduct a more formal assessment using PMI's *Organizational Project Management Maturity Model (OPM3®)* and related services.

X3.1 Questions Relating to Implementation of Critical Success Factors (See Section 2.1 – Assess Readiness for OPM Implementation)

X3.1.1 Sustained Leadership

- Who is the most senior, appropriately qualified person to sponsor a program fostering OPM?

- Who is the most senior, appropriately qualified person to lead OPM initiatives daily?

- What leadership network across the organization is best positioned to serve as a governance group or steering committee for OPM?

- What relevant current sponsorship practices are in place?

X3.1.2 Continuous Improvement

- What actions does the organization take to keep track of the achievements in organizational strategy? What success criteria are used?

- Who in the organization keeps track of the achievements in organizational strategy?

- How does the organization identify areas that need to be improved?

- How does the organization manage risk?

- Who in the organization defines the contingency plans?

- How does the organization identify opportunities (internal/external) that may help to achieve organizational strategy?

- How does the organization identify threats (internal/external) that may affect the achievement of organizational strategy?

- How often is a gap analysis conducted and when was the last one performed?

- Who in the organization defines the actions to be taken to achieve the organizational strategy?

- How are the organization's continuous improvement activities related to portfolios, programs, and projects?

X3.1.3 Organizational Change Management

- Do the business functional areas work in silos?

- How do the business functional areas in the organization perceive the support functions?

- How do the supporting functional areas in the organization perceive the business functional areas?

- What is the general perception of the supporting functional area?

- What is the general perception of the business functional area?

- Does the organization have cross-business functional area initiatives?

- Have the cross-business functional area initiatives been successful in the organization?

- What was the level of involvement of supporting functions in cross-functional initiatives?

- Does the organization link initiatives with business processes?

- How do projects fit into the cross-business initiatives in the organization?

- How do projects fit into the business processes?

- How does the organization manage change?

- Who leads change management in the organization?

- Does the organization have a change management process or policy?

- What communication channels exist for each type of stakeholder? How effective are these channels?

X3.2 Questions Relating to General Readiness for OPM Initiatives

- **Business results.** What is the current performance of contributing portfolios, programs, and projects?

- **Environmental factors.** How do the projects resonate with competitors, customers, or regulators?

- **Organizational culture and style.** What is the prevalent decision-making model? Is communication informal or formal? What is the organization's tolerance for risk? How results-oriented is the organization? What are the policies and practices relating to how employees are treated and encouraged to develop?

- **Organizational experience with substantial improvement changes.** How well does the organization handle change? Is the organization agile when it comes to change? What competing change initiatives could interfere with an OPM initiative?

- **Organizational process assets.** What is the governance process related to portfolios, programs, and projects? How does enterprise risk management fit the context of OPM? How effective is the project management information system? What other management systems require consideration?

- **Organizational strategic planning.** Is there a clear bridge from strategy, vision, and mission to the organization's programs and projects?

- **Organizational structures.** What are the existing related organizational structures or policies directing structure that may help or hinder an OPM implementation? Is the organization considered to be functional, matrix, or project-centric?

- **OPM-related roles and responsibilities.** Are there PMOs in place? Is there a formal or informal community of project management practice?

- **Previous organizational project management assessment results.** What credible knowledge exists regarding current capabilities and performance results relating to portfolios, programs, and projects?

- **Stakeholder list.** Who are the people in the organization that need to be on board for an OPM initiative? What will it take to get them there?

X3.3 Questions Relating to the Implementation of Core-Enabling Processes

X3.3.1 Strategic Alignment

- Does the organization have a documented strategic plan? Is it visible in yearly business plans?

- Do the business functional areas of the organization start projects independently without consulting the senior management team?

- Do all business and supporting functional area heads understand the purpose of the organization?

- How integrated are the business and supporting functional areas in the organization?

- Does the organization understand the benefit of aligning business and supporting functional areas to achieve the purpose of the organization?

- Do the supporting functional area heads understand what the business functional areas do for the organization?

- Do the business functional area heads understand what the supporting functional areas do for the organization?

- Do the employees of the organization understand what the supporting functional areas do for the organization?

- Do the employees of the organization understand what the business functional areas do for the organization?

X3.3.2 Organizational Project Management Methodology

- What is the level of project management knowledge in the business functional areas?

- What is the level of project management knowledge in the supporting area functions?

- When working together, do the business and supporting functional areas in the organization have a holistic approach to engaging portfolios, programs, and projects or do they focus on their own areas of expertise?

- Does the organization have a documented project management methodology of practices and techniques?

- What is the project management team's level of experience?

- Does the organization have a project management office? What services does it provide?

- How does the organization define success and failure metrics for projects?

X3.3.3 Governance

- Who in the organization approves major projects, for example, general manager/CEO, business functional area head (i.e., manager/director/vice president), or approval committee?

- Does the organization have a governance model/framework inclusive of portfolios, programs, and projects?

- If so, does the governance model/framework cascade through the business and supporting functional areas?

- If not, who in the organization identifies variances in the achievement of the organizational strategy?

- How often does the organization review the milestone achievements of the organizational strategy?

- Who belongs to the governance entity in the organization?

- How often does the governance entity meet?

X3.3.4 Competency Management

- Does the organization have formalized training and development plans for the business and supporting functional areas that support portfolio, program, and project management?

- Does the organization have a career development framework for the business and supporting functional areas that includes portfolio, program, and project management?

- How do the business and supporting functional areas share lessons learned that relate to improving the quality or efficiency of portfolios, programs, and projects?

- Does the organization support the creation and development of OPM-related communities of practice?

- How does the organization assess the skills of the management team and employees, related to portfolios, programs, and projects?

- Who in the organization is responsible for the professional development of the management team and employees in the areas of concern to OPM?

REFERENCES

[1] Project Management Institute. 2013. *Organizational Project Management Maturity Model (OPM3®)* – Third Edition. Newtown Square, PA: PMI.

[2] Project Management Institute. 2013. *PMI's Pulse of the Profession™: The High Cost of Low Performance.* Retrieved from www.PMI.org/pulse

[3] Project Management Institute. 2013. *Managing Organizational Change: A Practice Guide.* Newtown Square, PA: PMI.

[4] Thomas, J., and Mullaly, M. 2008. *Researching the Value of Project Management.* Newtown Square, PA: Project Management Institute.

[5] Project Management Institute. 2013. *The Standard for Program Management* – Third Edition. Newtown Square, PA: PMI.

[6] Project Management Institute. 2013. *A Guide to the Project Management Body of Knowledge (PMBOK® Guide)* – Fifth Edition. Newtown Square, PA: PMI.

[7] Project Management Institute. 2013. *The Standard for Portfolio Management* – Third Edition. Newtown Square, PA: PMI.

[8] Project Management Institute. 2012. *PMI Lexicon of Project Management Terms.* Newtown Square, PA: PMI.

[9] Project Management Institute. 2007. *Project Manager Competency Development Framework (PMCDF).* Newtown Square. PA: PMI.

ADDITIONAL RECOMMENDED READING

Aubry, M., Drouin, N., Jugdev, K., Muller, R., and Shao, J. 2012. *Organizational Enablers for Organizational Project Management.* Final Report, PMI Standards Program, Newtown Square, PA: Project Management Institute.

Bull, L., Shaw, K., Baca, C. 2012. "Delivering Strategy: Organizational Project Management and the Strategic PMO." PMI North American Congress, Vancouver.

Cooke-Davies, T. J., Crawford, L. H., and Lechler, T. 2008. Project Management Systems: Moving Project Management from an Operational to a Strategic Discipline. In *Proceedings of PMI Research Conference, Warsaw.* Newtown Square, PA: Project Management Institute.

Dinsmore, P. C., and Cooke-Davies, T. J. 2006. *The Right Projects Done Right! From Business Strategy to Successful Project Implementation.* San Francisco: John Wiley & Sons.

Mullaly, M., and Thomas, J. 2010. *Re-thinking Project Management Maturity: Perspectives Gained from Exploration of Fit and Value.* Newtown Square, PA: Project Management Institute

Project Management Institute. 2013. *Practice Standard for Project Risk Management.* Newtown Square, PA: Author.

Project Management Institute. 2012. *Executive Guide to Project Management.* Retrieved from www.PMI.org.

GLOSSARY

Capability. A specific competency that an organization needs to have in order to implement and sustain OPM.

Methodology. A system of practices, techniques, procedures, and rules used by those who work in a discipline.

Organization. An entity that may include all levels of the enterprise and may transcend business lines or divisions, including any area/business unit that has impact, influence, or involvement in project and business operations. The boundaries of an organization appropriate for OPM could vary by organization based on factors such as culture, size, maturity, and business needs. The principle is to include all aspects of project operations within an integrated framework.

Organizational Enablers. Organizational enablers are structural, cultural, technological, and human-resource practices that can be leveraged to support the implementation of Best Practices in portfolios, programs, and projects in support of strategic goals.

Organizational Project Management (OPM). OPM is a strategy execution framework utilizing portfolio, program, and project management as well as organizational-enabling practices to consistently and predictably deliver organizational strategy leading to better performance, better results, and a sustainable competitive advantage.

Organizational Process Assets. Plans, processes, policies, procedures, and knowledge bases that are specific to and used by the performing organization.

Organizational Project Management Maturity. The level of an organization's ability to deliver the desired strategic outcomes in a predictable, controllable, and reliable manner.

Organizational Project Management Methodology (OPM Methodology). A system of practices, techniques, procedures, and rules used by those who work in OPM. Project management methodology is a subset of OPM methodology.

Portfolio. Projects, programs, subportfolios, and operations managed as a group to achieve strategic objectives.

Portfolio Management. The centralized management of one or more portfolios to achieve strategic objectives.

Program. A group of related projects, subprograms, and program activities that are managed in a coordinated way to obtain benefits not available from managing them individually.

Program Management. The application of knowledge, skills, tools, and techniques to a program to meet the program requirements and to obtain benefits and control not available by managing projects individually.

Program Management Office. A management structure that standardizes the program-related governance processes and facilitates sharing of resources, methodologies, tools, and techniques.

Project. A temporary endeavor undertaken to create a unique product, service, or result.

Project Management. The application of knowledge, skills, tools, and techniques to project activities to meet the project requirements.

Project Management Methodology. A system of practices, techniques, procedures, and rules used by those who work in portfolios, programs, and projects. Project management methodology is a subset of OPM methodology.

Project Management Office. A management structure that standardizes the project-related governance processes and facilitates the sharing of resources, methodologies, tools, and techniques.

Sponsor. A person or group who provides resources and support for the portfolio, program, or project, and is accountable for enabling success.

Stakeholder. An individual, group, or organization who may affect, be affected by, or perceive itself to be affected by a decision, activity, or outcome of a portfolio, program, or project.

Sustainability. A characteristic of a process or state that can be maintained indefinitely.

INDEX